Wild Flowers of America

A PRODUCTION OF

DUENEWALD PRINTING CORPORATION

NEW YORK

Contents

Introduction

The four hundred paintings reproduced in this book are a selection from the beauty and interest of North American wild flowers. From the thousands of kinds of flowering plants which grow wild on the continent (and we do not yet know all of them), these were chosen for various reasons: some because they are hard to find — like those which frequent the upper slopes of the highest mountains; some because of their gorgeous colors or curious shapes — like Cardinal Flower and Lady's-slipper; some because everyone knows them — like Goldenrod and Buttercup. They range from the everlasting snows to tropic swamps, from woods to deserts. The Orchids, with their curious and often beautiful flowers, are well represented; so are those curious plants which catch insects and are nourished by them. Certain groups of exceptional beauty, like the Mariposa Lilies and the Gentians, are also fully treated.

In speaking of plants, the botanist finds it necessary to use technical names for them rather than the common names of spoken language; and the interested layman soon finds that it is best for him also to become familiar with botanical names, forbidding as they may seem at first sight. Plate 9, for instance, illustrates a plant commonly known as Western Red Cedar. The name Cedar has unfortunately been used for several trees superficially more or less alike but only distantly related. Western Red Cedar is closely related to Arbor Vitae, but not to the Red Cedar of the eastern states. The White Cedar is distinct from all these plants, and the Cedars of the Old World, including Cedar of Lebanon, are again only distantly related to them and do not even much resemble them. The Bluebells of Scotland (see Plate 365) are in a different family from English Bluebells, and neither is related to some of the many American plants called Bluebells (Plate 314, for example). The Spring Beauty of one midwestern state is called Hepatica in another, where the name Spring Beauty is used for a quite different flower. And so we might multiply examples of the confusion inherent in colloquial names, without even drawing attention to the fact that all such names are useless as soon as we pass into a country in which English is not spoken.

Botanical names are really quite simple; they are based on the classification of plants. All the plants of one sort which grow wild, form a population we call a species; all the white pines compose one species, all the limber pines another. Similar species, having certain main characters in common, form a genus; all pines — white, red, yellow, limber, and so on — are in one genus. Each genus (the plural is genera) has a name formed of a single word, usually a Latin noun: *Pinus, Rosa, Delphinium* are the names of genera. Many names of genera are in everyday use, especially by gardeners: *Begonia, Phlox, Gladiolus, Scilla, Narcissus, Chrysanthemum, Zinnia* are all names of genera. The name of a species is formed of two words, the first being the name of the genus to which it belongs, the second a qualifying word, usually a Latin adjective. *Pinus flexilis, Rosa carolina, Delphinium elongatum, Phlox divaricata* are the names of species. Within species the botanist often distinguishes groups set off by less evident differences (slight differences in form or color, for instance); such groups may be called subspecies, varieties, or forms, and are named by adding further qualifying words to the name of the species. Going in the other direction, we arrange genera in larger groups called families. Each family is named by a single word usually ending in -aceae: Pinaceae, Rosaceae, Geraniaceae are names of families. The families again compose the larger groups of the plant kingdom.

Two of these larger groups are represented in this book, the conifers and the flowering plants. The two groups are similar in many ways, the cones of the first resembling the flowers of the second in essential features; so that it is proper to include both in a work entitled *Wild Flowers of America*. The cones of conifers are composed of scales arranged spirally around a central stem. There are two kinds of cones. The scales of one kind form pollen in small sacs attached to their under surface; this pollen, when it is liberated in the spring, may appear as a visible yellow cloud. The scales which form pollen are called stamens, and the cones composed of stamens are staminate cones. They usually grow in clusters, and wither away after the pollen is shed (see Plates 7, 8).

The other kind of cone (Plates 1, 6) bears on its scales minute bodies called ovules, which, when fertilized by the pollen, become the seeds; these cones are called ovulate cones. As the seeds ripen, the cones become larger and usually more or less woody; the scales finally spread apart and the seeds attached to them fall out.

The essential parts of a flower are stamens and pistils; these are usually present in the same flower, though some species have distinct staminate and pistillate flowers. The stamens form pollen, like those of the conifers; each consists usually of an oblong head on a narrow stalk (well shown in Plates 30, 35). The stamens surround the pistil or pistils. The pistil consists of a hollow lower part, the ovary, which contains one or more ovules, and above this a style sup-

[7]

porting a stigma on which the pollen is deposited (or several styles and stigmas); the pistil is clearly seen in Plates 30 and 274. These parts are in most flowers surrounded by the perianth, which is composed commonly of two rings or cycles of parts, an outer ring of sepals, which are often green, and an inner ring of petals, which may be brightly colored and of complex form (see, for instance, the Trillium in Plate 55). However, the two rings of parts may be all alike or nearly so, as in the Lily shown in Plate 32, in which case the terms sepals and petals are not used; or there may be only one ring of parts, as in the Anemone shown in Plate 120, in which case they are arbitrarily called sepals.

All the parts of the flower are attached to the tip of the flower-stalk, which is commonly expanded into a knob, a disc, or a cup, and is referred to as the receptacle. When it is cup-shaped or urn-shaped, as in a Rose (see Plate 184), the pistil or pistils occupy the inside of the cup, the stamens and perianth being attached to its margin. In many flowers the ovary is not only within a cup-shaped receptacle, it is so embedded in it that it cannot be detached; one cannot say where the ovary leaves off and the receptacle begins. This sort of ovary is spoken of as inferior. It is not easy to demonstrate in a painting of a flower, but in Blue-eyed Grass (Plate 63) it may be seen that the tip of the flower-stalk is swollen just below the blue perianth; this part contains the inferior ovary.

The pollen received by the stigma sends its pollen tubes into the pistil and fertilizes the ovules therein.

As the ovules develop into seeds, the surrounding ovary also enlarges and changes in structure, becoming the fruit. This is the essential difference between cones and flowers: in cones the seeds are attached to the surface of the parts that bear them; in flowers they are enclosed in a hollow structure. Other parts of the flower may be involved in the formation of the fruit, particularly if the ovary is inferior.

The first two families treated in this book are conifers; the rest are flowering plants.

The brief descriptions which follow are intended to call attention to the principal features which distinguish a species from its relatives; except those which are clearly evident in the illustrations. It is obviously impossible, without a much more detailed and technical treatment, to provide a means of identification for all North American wild flowers. The heights given are usually the maximum heights to which the species may grow; but when this is shown in the paintings (which are all life-size) it is not mentioned in the descriptions. The plants come from all over the North American continent north of Mexico (and a few extend south of the boundary). Some idea is given of the habitat of each species, that is, the kind of situation in which it is found. Some plants are so widely distributed that it is difficult to say anything of their preferences in soil, moisture and shade. Others are designated simply as "arctic," which means that they grow where the ground is frozen most of the year; or "alpine," when they frequent the rocky slopes or mountain meadows above timberline.

— H. W. RICKETT

The Mary Vaux Walcott color plates in this book are reproduced by permission from the famous portfolio set "North American Wild Flowers," by Mary Vaux Walcott, as published by the Smithsonian Institution.

[8]

Glossary

Achene: A small dry fruit containing one seed, and not splitting open at maturity; see Buttercup, Sunflower.

Basal: At the base; of leaves growing at the base of the stem, as those of Saxifrage; of the lower parts of petals, sepals, etc.

Beard: A tuft of hairs, as on the petal of Pogonia.

Berry: A fruit which is succulent throughout, as Grape, Tomato.

Bracts: Leaves associated with flowers, usually smaller than the other leaves, as in Phlox, Tar-flower; often differently shaped or colored, as in *Monarda, Castilleia;* also associated with the scales of ovulate cones.

Bud-scales: Scales which enclose a dormant bud, usually falling when the bud opens.

Capsule: A pod containing seeds enclosed in several chambers or attached in several rows, and splitting open into several parts at maturity; found in Lilies, Violets, and many others.

Catkin: An often pendent branch of small flowers which usually lack petals and either stamens or pistils, as in Willows and Alders.

Chaff: In this book, applied to the bracts associated with the disc-flowers of the Composite Family; see p. 59.

Claw: The narrow stalk by which some petals are attached; see *Lilium umbellatum.*

Column: The peculiar structure in the center of an orchid flower, composed of style, stigma and one or two stamens joined together; see p. 20.

Corm: A bulbous underground stem, as in Trillium.

Crest: A ridge or protrusion, especially on petals, as in Milkwort, Squirrel Corn.

Crown: A ring formed by outgrowths from the perianth, as in Daffodils (where it forms the "trumpet") and Milkweed.

Epiphyte: A plant which grows attached to another plant but does not draw its nourishment from it, as *Epidendrum.*

Falls: See p. 20.

Gland: A body which exudes some substance, such as oil or nectar; also used of bodies which have the appearance of glands.

Glaucous: Grayish-green with a waxy surface.

Inferior ovary: An ovary imbedded in the receptacle; see p. 8.

Involucre: A circle of bracts usually beneath a flower-cluster, as in *Anemone deltoidea, Pulsatilla,* the Composite Family.

Irregular flower: A flower which is not radially symmetrical, the upper parts differing from the lower; see the Orchid and Mint Families.

Keel: The two lower petals of the flower of the Bean Family, joined by their lower edges to form a boat-shaped body; also a similar body in the flower of Milkwort.

Lip: The lower petal of an orchid flower, usually much larger than the others and of a different shape; see also two-lipped.

Nectar: A sweet liquid formed in flowers.

Nectar-gland, nectary: A body which exudes nectar, found in various positions in flowers.

Ovary: The lower part of a pistil, which contains the ovules; see p. 7.

Ovule: The rudiment of a seed.

Palate: A projection on the lower lip of some two-lipped flowers which closes the opening or nearly so, as in Toadflax.

Palmately: Spreading like the fingers of a hand; referring to leaf-segments, as those of Lupine, Buckeye.

Papilionaceous: Butterfly-like; referring to the type of flower characteristic of the Bean Family (p. 37).

Pappus: A structure which replaces sepals in the individual flowers of the Composite Family; often composed of small scales or bristles (see p. 59).

Parasite: A plant (or animal) which is attached to another plant (or animal) and takes its nourishment directly from it, as Mistletoe, Cancer-root.

Perianth: The part of a flower which surrounds the stamens and pistil; its parts are of a great variety of shapes, often brightly colored; see p. 8.

Pinnately: Arranged in two ranks along the sides of a stalk, as the leaf-segments of Vetch, Mountain Ash.

Pistil: The central part of a flower (or there may be several); the lower part usually enlarges and forms the case (fruit) around the seeds; see p. 7.

Plumose: Feathery.

Pod: A dry fruit which opens when ripe; capsule.

Pollen: A dust-like or sticky mass made up of minute grains, commonly yellow, formed in the head of a stamen (see p. 7).

Pollinium: A mass of cohering pollen grains found in Orchids and Milkweeds.

Pseudobulb: A thickened branch of an Orchid containing food and water.

Receptacle: The end of the flower-stalk to which the parts of the flower are attached; often expanded, cup-shaped in a Cherry blossom, urn-shaped in a Rose, cushion-like in a Strawberry.

Sepals: The outer parts of the perianth when this is composed of two rings, as in Buttercups; equivalent to perianth when the parts of the latter are all alike, as in Anemone; see p. 8.

Spadix: The thick branch on which the flowers of the Arum Family are borne (p. 13).

Spathe: The large bract which encloses the spadix of the Arum Family (p. 13); also used of any large bract or group of bracts, as in Blue-eyed Grass.

Spur: A hollow projection or tubular extension usually of a petal, as in Violet, Columbine.

Stamen: The part of a flower which forms the pollen; the stamens are situated within the perianth and around the pistil or pistils; each consists commonly of a stalk and head; see p. 7.

Standard: The upper petal of the characteristic flower of the Bean Family; also a sepal of an Iris.

Stellate: Star-shaped, having radiating arms; many plant hairs, as those of Bladderpod, Scarlet Globe-mallow, may be seen through a magnifier to have radiating branches.

Stigma: The uppermost part of the pistil, which receives the pollen.

Stipules: Paired appendages, often like small leaves or leaf-segments, at the base of a leaf-stalk; as in Rose.

Style: The slender part of the pistil which rises from the ovary and bears the stigma.

Tendril: A slender clasping or coiling structure, usually a special branch or a part of a leaf, by which some plants attach themselves to supporting objects; see Vetch.

Tuber: An underground enlarged stem or root or portion thereof in which food, such as starch or sugar, accumulates; see Rue Anemone.

Tubercle: A small enlargement, as at the base of the hairs of some Sunflowers.

Two-lipped: Petals or sepals which are united to form a tube may spread at the end into unequal upper and lower lips; see *Chelone, Monarda*.

Umbel: A flower-cluster, roughly resembling an umbrella, in which all the stalks radiate from one point; see Bird's-eye Primrose.

Valve: One of the parts into which a capsule splits at maturity.

Whorl: A ring or cycle of parts; referring to leaves, petals, etc.

Wing: A flattened extension of a fruit, as in Maples; one of the lateral petals of the papilionaceous flower of the Bean Family.

Conifers. Coniferae

Pine family. Pinaceae

Pl. 1. Alpine Fir *Abies lasiocarpa*

The firs may be distinguished by their erect cones. Their leaves are mostly flat and blunt, without stalks; when they fall, they leave the branches smooth. The bark forms abundant liquid resin in blister-like pockets.

Alpine Fir is a pyramidal tree reaching 100 feet and more in height, with leaves 1 to 1¾ inches long. The cones are 2½ to 4 inches long when mature. The wood is light, weak, of little value.

A related species is the Balsam Fir of the northeastern states, much used for Christmas trees.

Alpine Fir grows on high mountain slopes up to timberline, from Montana to Washington and Alaska, and southward to northern New Mexico and Arizona. The specimen illustrated came from Bow Pass, near the boundary of Alberta and British Columbia, at an altitude of 6,000 feet.

Pl. 2. Engelmann Spruce
Picea engelmanni

Most spruces have leaves four-sided in cross section, stiff and sharply pointed. Each leaf grows from a minute woody pedestal which remains on the branch after the leaf has fallen; these give spruce branches their characteristic roughness.

This species is a tall tree (reaching 150 feet and more in height), with rather flexible leaves 1 to 1⅛ inches long. Its pendent cones are 1 to 3 inches long. The wood is light, soft, and of limited usefulness as lumber.

Engelmann Spruce grows at high altitudes — up to 8,000 feet in Oregon, and not often below 2,500 feet — from the Rocky Mountains in Alberta and British Columbia westward to the Cascade Mountains, and southward to New Mexico, Arizona and northern California. The branch illustrated grew in the Clearwater River Valley, Alberta, at an altitude of 7,000 feet.

Pl. 3. Mountain Hemlock
Tsuga mertensiana

The leaves of hemlocks are flat and grow on tiny stalks; these commonly twist so as to bring all the leaves nearly into one plane, which give the branches a characteristic fan-like appearance; in this species however, the leaves are arranged in star-like clusters. The cones are relatively small and often very numerous.

The Mountain Hemlock is a narrow spire-like tree, reaching 100 feet in height, with leaves ½ to 1 inch long. The cones are ½ to 3 inches long, hanging from the ends of the branches, often in dense clusters. The wood is soft and of no value.

Mountain Hemlock grows at high altitudes, often associated with Alpine Fir, from Montana to Alaska and southward to California. Other species of *Tsuga* are common in the eastern and southern states. The specimen illustrated came from Glacier, British Columbia, at an altitude of 3,500 feet.

Pl. 4. Douglas Fir *Pseudotsuga taxifolia*

This tree is called the false hemlock (Pseudotsuga) because its leaves are stalked like those of hemlocks and its cones droop from the ends of the branches. It has also been called fir because of its pitch-pockets, and spruce because of the arrangement of its leaves. In the structure of its cones, however, it differs from all these trees. A distinctive feature is the two-lobed, long-pointed bracts which project between the seed-bearing scales.

This species is a large tree, often reaching 200 feet in height (and sometimes over 300 feet), with soft, flat leaves ¾ to 1¼ inches long. The cones are 2 to 4 inches long. It is a valuable source of lumber.

Douglas Fir grows from sea level to high altitudes, from Wyoming southward to western Texas and northern Mexico, and westward to the Pacific Coast in British Columbia, Washington and Oregon and to the Sierra Nevada in California (but absent from the dry mountain ranges of the Great Basin). The illustration was made from a branch obtained near Radium Hot Springs in the Columbia River Valley, British Columbia, at an altitude of 3,000 feet.

Pl. 5. Western Larch *Larix occidentalis*

Larches differ from other conifers in shedding their leaves every winter. The short, needle-like leaves grow in clusters on spur-like shoots which arise from the branches.

This species may reach 200 feet in height; the branches are long and slender. The leaves are 1 to 2 inches long, 3-angled in section, from 14 to 30 in a cluster. The cones are small (1 to 1½ inches long) and grow thickly along the branches.

A related species is the Tamarack of northeastern swampy forests.

Western Larch grows at altitudes of 2,000 to 7,000 feet from Montana to British Columbia and southward to northern Idaho, northeastern Oregon and the Columbia River. The branch illustrated came from Horse Thief River, British Columbia, at an altitude of 3,000 feet.

PINE *PINUS*

The pines are distinguished by having their leaves in small clusters on spur-like lateral shoots, much as the larches do; the needles are longer than those of the larches and fewer in a cluster, and remain on the tree for several years. They are our most valuable sources of lumber. There are many species, occurring all over the northern hemisphere.

Pl. 6. Limber Pine *Pinus flexilis*

This is usually a small tree or even a shrub, stunted by the rigorous conditions of the high mountains where it grows. The leaves grow 5 to a spur and are 2 to 3 inches long. The cones are 4 to 10 inches long. The illustration shows, at the extreme tip of the branch, young ovulate cones ready for pollen; as the branch continues its growth, these will bend aside and grow to be like the year-old cone below.

Limber Pine grows near timberline from South Dakota to Alberta and southward to western Texas, New Mexico and California. The specimen sketched grew near Lake Minnewonka, Alberta, at an altitude of 4,000 feet.

Pl. 7. Long-leaved Pine *Pinus palustris*

This tree grows from 100 to 120 feet tall. The wood is hard, strong and coarse, much valued for lumber, turpentine and resin. The leaves are 8 to 18 inches long. The cones are 6 to 10 inches long.

Long-leaved Pine is found in wet ground mainly on the coastal plain from southern Virginia to Florida and westward as far as eastern Texas. Plate 7 shows a cluster of staminate cones. The specimen came from Ladies Island near Beaufort, South Carolina.

Pl. 8. Loblolly Pine *Pinus taeda*

Loblolly Pine is a tall tree growing from 80 to 100 feet in height. The wood, although weak, is used commercially. The leaves of this species are short and stiff, 6 to 9 inches long. The cones are 2 to 6 inches long.

It is found in sandy soil and old fields from New Jersey to Florida and westward to western Louisiana and eastern Texas.

A cluster of staminate cones is shown in the figure. The specimen came from Beaufort, South Carolina.

Cypress family. Cupressaceae

Pl. 9. Western Red Cedar *Thuja plicata*

Unfortunately the name Cedar has been given to several trees superficially alike but only distantly related botanically. Western Red Cedar is related to Arbor Vitae but is not in the same genus as Eastern Red Cedar; the latter is a species of *Juniperus*. Besides these, the White Cedar of the eastern states is still another genus. The true Cedars of the Old World are *Cedrus*. The name Western Red Cedar is applied also to another western species, *Juniperus occidentalis*. All of which demonstrates the unreliability of common names and the necessity for scientific nomenclature.

The leaves of *Thuja plicata* are scale-like, covering the branchlets in 4 rows. The cones are very small; the seed cones are only half an inch long when mature, as pictured in Plate 9.

The tree grows to a height of 200 feet. The wood is light in weight and soft and is used in cabinet work and interior finish. Indians made much use of the wood for building canoes and lodges and of the fibrous bark for blankets and thatch.

It is found in the coastal ranges of Oregon and California, northward into British Columbia, and eastward to Idaho and Montana, from sea level to 7,000 feet.

Pl. 10. Creeping Juniper
Juniperus horizontalis

In the Junipers, the 2 to 6 scales of the minute cones grow together to form a fleshy structure which is commonly called a berry, as is clearly seen in Plate 11. The leaves are needle-like, being only ¼ to ½ inch long. As the name indicates, this plant grows close to the ground. Several forms are cultivated in rock gardens.

Creeping Juniper is found at altitudes up to 5,000 feet, from Newfoundland to northern New York and westward to Alaska, Wyoming and Nebraska. The plant shown came from the Saskatchewan River in Alberta, at an altitude of 5,000 feet.

Pl. 11. Mountain Juniper *Juniperus sibirica*

This Juniper is sometimes called *Juniperus communis* variety *saxatilis*. Each leaf is marked with a white line; the plant is more or less trailing. The berries are small, from 1/3 to ½ inch in diameter.

Juniperus sibirica occurs from Labrador to Alaska and southward to Nova Scotia, Maine, Wisconsin, Wyoming and California. The specimen shown came from the Saskatchewan River Valley in British Columbia at an altitude of 4,000 feet.

Flowering Plants. Angiospermae

Water-plantain family. Alismataceae

Pl. 12. Arrowleaf *Sagittaria cuneata*

On each flowering stalk the lower flowers are usually pistillate, the upper staminate. There are 3 sepals, 3 white petals, and many stamens and pistils in each flower. The pistils become small seed-like fruits crowded in a dense globular head. This species sometimes grows submerged, and then instead of arrow-shaped leaves, ribbon-like leaves are formed.

This Arrowleaf (there are several other species) grows in wet places from Nova Scotia and Quebec to New Jersey and westward to British Columbia, California and New Mexico. The specimen used for the painting came from Edgewater, British Columbia, at an altitude of 2,700 feet.

Sedge family. Cyperaceae

This family contains the sedges, grass-like plants with inconspicuous greenish or brownish flowers. The stems are usually solid and triangular in cross section, and the leaf blades spring from sheaths which completely enclose the stem; whereas in the grasses the stem is often hollow and round, and the leaf sheath is open down one side.

Pl. 13. Cotton Grass

Eriophorum chamissonis

Various species of Cotton Grass are familiar in bogs and moors, often high in the mountains, all over the northern hemisphere. The soft white bristles represent the perianth (sepals and petals) of other flowers.

This species grows from Labrador to New Brunswick and westward to Alaska and Oregon. The plant sketched grew near Lake Louise, Alberta, at an altitude of 7,000 feet.

Pl. 14. Golden Sedge *Carex aurea*

The enormous genus *Carex* includes over 500 species in North America alone, and is abundant all over the world, chiefly in the cooler parts. The tiny flowers lack recognizable sepals and petals; they stand next to scales, in small clusters called spikelets; the stamens and pistils are in separate flowers, and these are often in different parts of the flower cluster. The pistils become small seed-like fruits, which are enveloped by a special covering. In the Golden Sedge this special envelope is golden brown, and, with the brownish-green scales, imparts a golden color to the oval spikelets.

Golden Sedge grows in wet places from Newfoundland to Connecticut and westward to British Columbia, California and New Mexico. The specimen illustrated was found in the valley of the Siffleur River, Alberta, at an altitude of 5,000 feet.

Arum family. Araceae

The Arum family has numerous small flowers, sometimes lacking sepals and petals, closely packed on a stalk called the spadix, which is often thick and fleshy; around the spadix usually extends a sheathing leaf or spathe, often colored and mistaken for a petal. Most species of the family are tropical.

Pl. 15. Jack-in-the-pulpit, Indian Turnip

Arisaema triphyllum

"Jack" is the upper part of the spadix; the "pulpit" is the spathe. The flowers are on the lower part of the spadix; the pistillate flowers form the red berries which are visible when the spathe withers away.

The underground stem (corm) was eaten by the Indians *after being thoroughly boiled;* in the raw state it causes an intense burning sensation of the mouth, which lasts for a long time.

Jack-in-the-pulpit grows in woods and wet places from Nova Scotia to Florida, and westward to Minnesota and Louisiana. The plant used for illustration grew in Bryn Mawr, Pennsylvania.

Pl. 16. Green Dragon *Arisaema dracontium*

In this species the spadix is prolonged into a slender tapering horn which protrudes from the spathe. Each leaf is divided into from 5 to 15 segments instead of the 3 found in *Arisaema triphyllum*.

Green Dragon grows in damp woods from Quebec to Florida and westward to Minnesota and Texas; it is less common than Jack-in-the-pulpit. The plant sketched was found near Washington, D. C.

Pl. 17. Wild Calla *Calla palustris*

As in the familiar Calla Lily, the spathe of this plant is white and may be mistaken for a single petal. The true flowers, however, are the small objects which cover the entire surface of the spadix.

Wild Calla frequents cold bogs and shallow water from Newfoundland to Florida and westward to

Alaska, Minnesota, Colorado and Texas. The illustration was made from a plant growing near Sudbury, Ontario.

Pl. 18 Skunk Cabbage
Symplocarpus foetidus

Skunk Cabbage grows usually in mud or shallow water, beneath the surface of which the flowers are formed in the autumn; they usually push up to the air early in spring, before the leaves unfold. The flowers cover the thick short spadix; each is four-angled, and the parts are in fours. The fruits are embedded in the spadix, which becomes large and spongy. The odor attracts flies, which help to carry the pollen from one flower to another.

The range of Skunk Cabbage is wide, from Nova Scotia and Quebec to Florida and westward to Minnesota and Iowa. The specimen illustrated came from Washington, D. C.

Pl. 19. Golden Club *Orontium aquaticum*

The "golden club" is the spadix covered by the yellow flowers; it is not enveloped in the spathe, which in this species is merely a sheath around its stalk. Gnats and other small insects frequent the flowers.

Golden Club grows in swamps and shallow water from Massachusetts to Florida and westward to central New York, Kentucky and Louisiana. The plant shown grew in Beaufort, South Carolina.

Spiderwort family.
Commelinaceae

Pl. 20. Spiderwort *Tradescantia virginiana*

Like those of the Lily Family, the flowers have parts mostly in threes and sixes. The 3 petals are blue, purple or rose, or occasionally white; they soon wither away. Below the flower-cluster is a pair of leaf-like bracts, usually unequal in length. The common name is derived from the narrow stiff leaves which project on all sides of the flower-cluster like so many legs.

A relative of this genus, often a creeping pest in gardens, is *Commelina,* the common Day Flower, whose 2 upper petals are sky-blue.

Spiderwort grows in prairies, roadsides and thickets from Maine to Georgia and westward to Minnesota, Missouri and Tennessee. The plant illustrated grew near Washington, D. C.

Pickerel Weed family.
Pontederiaceae

Pl. 21. Pickerel Weed *Pontederia cordata*

As the common name indicates, the plant grows in water, with the lustrous green leaves and spikes of pale blue or lavender flowers emerging from the surface. Each flower has a perianth of 6 parts, all much alike in color, the upper 3 joined to form an upper lip. There are 6 stamens. The ovary has 3 chambers, but only one forms a seed.

Pickerel Weed grows from Nova Scotia to Florida and westward to Minnesota and Texas. The plant shown in the painting came from Washington, D. C.

Pineapple family.
Bromeliaceae

The Bromeliads are mostly air plants; that is, they grow attached to the branches of trees and have no direct connection with the ground. They are not parasites, for they do not obtain food from the supporting plant. Such a habit of life is limited to warm humid regions; air plants are most abundant in the tropics. Other members of the family are the pineapple and the Spanish Moss (not a moss but a flowering plant) which hangs from the trees so abundantly in our southern states.

Pl. 22. Tillandsia *Tillandsia fasciculata*

This Tillandsia (there are over 100 species of the genus) may be distinguished from others by the long rigid leaves with their edges inrolled. It has narrow blue flowers in a spike covered with red-tinged scales (bracts).

It grows in southern Florida, and in the West Indies and Central America. The plant illustrated was found in a hammock near West Palm Beach, Florida.

Lily family. Liliaceae

The Lily Family supplies us with many familiar flowers — Lilies, Hyacinths, Tulips, Lilies-of-the-valley, Onions, Asparagus, and many others. All are characterized by flowers with a perianth of 6 segments (often in 2 sets of 3, but usually all colored alike), 6 stamens, and a 3-chambered ovary which is never wholly inferior. The fruit may be a pod or a berry. Many species grow from bulbs or underground stems; but a few, such as the Joshua Tree, are tree-like.

Pl. 23. Bear-grass *Xerophyllum tenax*

Many plants are known as grass which do not belong to the Grass Family, mostly because they resemble grass in having narrow leaves. The dense cluster of leaves of Bear-grass arises at the base of a flowering stem which may grow five feet high. The individual flowers are liliaceous, small, crowded.

The species grows in high mountain meadows and open woods from the Rocky Mountains to the Cascade Mountains of Washington and Oregon, and in northern California. The specimen illustrated grew in

Mount Rainier National Park, Washington.

Pl. 24. Glaucous Zygadene
Zygadenus elegans

The word glaucous refers to the blue-green color of the leaves, which is caused by a fine waxy coating. The name Zygadenus is derived from the Greek and alludes to the glands on the segments of the perianth; in this species they are heart-shaped. The ovary is partly inferior, and is crowned by 3 separate styles.

Death Camass, so called because of its poisonous bulb, is *Zygadenus venenosus*.

Glaucous Zygadene grows in moist meadows from Colorado to Nevada and Oregon and northward to Alaska. The plant sketched came from the Clearwater River, British Columbia, at an altitude of 6,500 feet.

Pl. 25. False Hellebore *Veratrum viride*

The small flowers of this species are inconspicuous and often missed, but the clusters of large bright green leaves are often striking in spring in swampy places and wet woods. The leaves are strongly ribbed and folded or pleated lengthwise. The underground stem is poisonous.

The name Veratrum was anciently applied to the Hellebore (the so-called Christmas Rose). False Hellebore resembles the true Hellebore only in the greenish cast of its flowers.

The species has a wide range from New Brunswick to Georgia and westward to Alaska, the Cascade Mountains, and northern California. The plant shown in the painting grew in the Bow Valley, Alberta, at an altitude of 6,500 feet.

Pl. 26. Fly-poison
Amianthium muscaetoxicum

Amianthium is distinguished from *Zygadenus* by the lack of glands on the perianth, and from *Camassia* by its 3 styles and stigmas. The bulb is very poisonous and has been used in the preparation of a fly-poison. The plant may reach a height of 4 feet.

It grows in open woods from Long Island to Florida and westward to Arkansas. The plant illustrated was found near Washington, D. C.

Pl. 27. Camass *Camassia quamash*

Several kinds of Camass are common in moist meadows of the Pacific states and the Rocky Mountains, and one in open woodlands of the Midwest. *Camassia quamash* is distinguished by the deep blue color and the slight irregularity of the perianth: 5 of the perianth parts grow upward, leaving the lowermost extending downward by itself. The ovary supports a single style. The plant reaches a height of 2 feet. The bulbs were valued as food by the Indians, who gave them the name "quamash."

This Camass grows from Montana and Utah to British Columbia and southward along the Coast Ranges to California. The plant sketched was found in Glacier National Park, Montana.

DOG-TOOTH VIOLET, ADDER'S-TONGUE
ERYTHRONIUM

The flowering stem of these plants arises, with the pair of leaves which envelop it, from a bulb deep under the surface. The bulb may propagate itself by sending out slender runners at the tips of which new bulbs are formed. Plants which have not yet reached flowering age (which may require severals years) have only a single leaf. The nodding flowers, one or several on a stalk in a variety of colors, closely resemble small lilies; the fruit is a small 3-angled pod.

The name *Erythronium* is derived from a Greek word meaning red. The European species has a reddish-purple flower. The word violet was once applied to any spring flower. Adder's-tongue seems to allude to the mottled leaves of some species, which suggest snake-skin.

Pl. 28. White Adder's-tongue, Dog-tooth
Violet *Erythronium albidum*

This is the common species of the Midwest, growing in meadows and open woodlands, often in rocky soil. Its flowers are solitary, and vary in color from cream-white to bluish. The style is 3-cleft at the tip, with 3 stigmas. The leaves are usually, but not always, mottled.

White Adder's-tongue grows from southern Ontario to Georgia and westward to Minnesota, Missouri and Oklahoma. The plant illustrated was found in the Potomac Valley.

Pl. 29. Yellow Adder's-tongue, Dog-tooth
Violet *Erythronium americanum*

Yellow Adder's-tongue is common in the Atlantic states, growing in the rich loam of open woods. The flowers are solitary. The stamens may be of 2 sizes, 3 of each size, and they vary in color in different races. The style is not cleft and the one stigma is 3-lobed. The leaves are mottled.

Erythronium americanum is found from Nova Scotia to Florida and westward to Minnesota and Oklahoma (becoming scarcer as one goes westward). The painting was made near Washington, D. C.

Pl. 30. Avalanche Lily
Erythronium montanum

Avalanche Lily grows on high mountain slopes, often appearing at the edge of the melting snow in spring or even growing up through the snow. There may be several flowers on a stalk. The stigma is 3-parted. The leaves are green, not mottled.

Erythronium montanum is found only in Washington and Oregon. The plant sketched grew in Paradise Valley on the slopes of Mount Rainier, Washington.

Pl. 31. Glacier Lily
Erythronium grandiflorum

Glacier Lilies grow in open forests and grassy mountain-sides in the Rocky Mountains and the Cascades.

[15]

They may have several flowers to a stalk. The anthers are reddish-purple. The style is 3-cleft at the tip, with 3 stigmas. The leaves are not mottled. There is also a white-flowered form.

They range from Wyoming to British Columbia and southward to California in the Cascade Mountains. The plant used for the painting was found near Field, British Columbia, at an altitude of 6,000 feet.

LILY *LILIUM*

The large genus *Lilium* needs little introduction. It grows in many parts of the world — Asia, Europe and North America. The plants are mostly tall and leafy, with large flowers of all shades of white, yellow, orange and red. The numerical pattern of the family is clearly seen in these flowers — 6 perianth parts all more or less alike in color, 6 stamens, and a 3-chambered ovary which becomes a 3-sided pod. The stigma is 3-lobed. The flower may have the form of a funnel, or the parts of the perianth may be reflexed as in the familiar Tiger-lily. The flowering stems arise from an underground scaly bulb or rootstock.

Pl. 32. Canada Lily *Lilium canadense*
Canada Lily grows in moist meadows, reaching heights of over 6 feet. The leaves form circles or whorls, and are rather rough to the touch. The perianth is either yellow or orange, usually marked with brown spots.

Canada Lily occurs from Nova Scotia to Georgia and Alabama and inland to Minnesota, Nebraska and Missouri. The plant illustrated grew in Bryn Mawr, Pennsylvania.

Pl. 33. Turk's-cap Lily *Lilium superbum*
The Turk's-cap may grow 7 feet high or more. The leaves are smooth. The lower form whorls, and the upper are scattered. This Lily grows in rich low grounds from New Brunswick to Florida and westward to Minnesota, Missouri and Tennessee. The plant sketched grew near Washington, D. C.

Pl. 34. Columbia Lily *Lilium columbianum*
Columbia Lily grows from a small bulb (up to 2 inches across) and reaches a height of 4 feet. The lower leaves form whorls, the upper are scattered.

The species is found in moist open woods and meadows from British Columbia to central California, and eastward to Idaho. The painting was made in Mount Rainier National Park, at an altitude of 2,000 feet.

Pl. 35. Western Red Lily
Lilium umbellatum
The Western Red Lily is a close relative of the Wood Lily of the eastern states, *Lilium philadelphicum,* and is sometimes classified as a variety of that species. Both are distinguished by their brilliant color and by having their perianth parts tapering at the base to narrow claws. *Lilium umbellatum* grows about

3 feet high. Its leaves are scattered and rather narrow (those of *Lilium philadelphicum* are broader and form whorls).

Lilium umbellatum grows in wet meadows from Ontario to British Columbia and southward to Ohio, and along the Rocky Mountains to New Mexico. The painting was made near Radium Hot Springs, British Columbia, at an altitude of 3,000 feet.

MARIPOSA LILY *CALOCHORTUS*

There are about 50 kinds of Mariposa Lilies, natives of western North America. The leaves and flowering stalks arise from small underground stems known as corms. There are only a few flowers to a plant, often only one. They have extraordinary variety and charm, ranging in color from white to blue, purple, yellow, orange, and even red. There are 3 broad concave petals, with a gland at the base which is frequently of a contrasting color and texture; 3 often narrow and variously colored sepals; 6 stamens; and the 3-chambered ovary characteristic of the family, which becomes a small pod. The generic name is derived from two Greek words meaning beautiful grass.

Pl. 36. Catalina Mariposa
Calochortus catalinae
The petals of this species vary from almost white to deep lilac; the sepals are spotted with purple near the base. The pod is blunt, obtuse-angled, up to 2 inches long.

Catalina Mariposa was so named because it was discovered on Santa Catalina Island, off southern California. It is found also in other islands of the Santa Barbara group and on the neighboring mainland. The painting was made at Santa Ana.

Pl. 37. Lilac Mariposa
Calochortus splendens
The stems of the Lilac Mariposa are branched, with a flower at the end of each branch. Long tangled hairs grow sparsely from the lilac or purple petals. The pod is narrow and may be over 2 inches long.

The species is found on dry stony hills, often in the low brush called chaparral, in the coast ranges of southern California. The plant illustrated grew at Santa Ana.

Pl. 38. Cat's Ear *Calochortus elegans*
The flowers are borne near the ground, with the basal leaf usually extending high above them. Sepals are greenish-white, often tinged with purple; petals are white tinged with purple and densely hairy — whence the common name. The sharply 3-angled short pod hangs down at the end of its stalk.

Cat's Ear grows from the eastern slopes of the Cascade Mountains in British Columbia and Washington eastward to Montana and Utah. The plant illustrated was found in the Columbia River Valley near Canal Flats, British Columbia, at an altitude of 2,500 feet.

Pl. 39 Green-banded Mariposa, Star Tulip *Calochortus macrocarpus*

Green-banded Mariposa grows rather tall, up to 2 feet in height, and forms bulbs at its base. The long narrow sepals are tinged with purple; the petals are purple with a yellow base and a green band down the middle, and bear sparse yellow hairs at the base. The pod is long-pointed and slender, with narrow wings at the angles.

It grows in dry places from Montana to British Columbia and southward on the eastern slopes of the Cascade Mountains to northern California. The plant illustrated was found near Canal Flats in British Columbia, at an altitude of 3,500 feet.

Pl. 40. Golden Bowl *Calochortus clavatus*

The stem is zigzag, branched, and up to 3 feet tall, with the flowers in a cluster. The sepals are rather broad and yellowish; the yellow petals bear hairs which are club-shaped. The 3-inch pod is long-pointed.

Golden Bowl grows on wooded slopes in southern California.

Pl. 41. Red Mariposa *Calochortus kennedyi*

The brilliant red flowers of this species are unique in the genus; even the sepals and flower-stalks are reddish. The narrow 2-inch pod tapers to a point, and is often striped with purplish at the angles.

Red Mariposa is found on dry hills of the desert region from southern Nevada to Arizona and westward to California.

Pl. 42. Weed's Mariposa *Calochortus weedii*

There may be from 1 to 4 flowers at the ends of as many stiff branches. The sepals are yellow like the petals, both more or less marked with fine brown lines; the petals are softly hairy. The pod is narrow and tapering.

Weed's Mariposa grows on dry hills in San Diego County, California, where the painting was made.

Pl. 43. Blue Dicks *Dichelostemma pauciflorum*

The delicate leaves and flowering stem of Blue Dicks appear in early spring in desert regions; the deep bulb lives from year to year through the long periods of drought. The bulbs were eaten by the Indians. In aspect (but not in odor) this and related genera somewhat resemble the Wild Onions. It is readily distinguished from similar plants by the stamens; 3 of the 6 have wing-like appendages. This species is sometimes classified as a variety of the California Blue Dicks, *Dichelostemma capitatum*.

The species grows in Arizona and New Mexico (*Dichelostemma capitatum* grows in California and Oregon and southward into northern Mexico). The painting was made near Tucson, Arizona.

Pl. 44. Wild Onion *Allium cernuum*

There are about 300 species of Wild Onions, widely distributed over the world; of these about 50 grow in North America — most of them in California. The onion of kitchen and table is the bulb, a short underground stem crowned with closely overlapped scaly leaves; from the center of the stem arises the flowering stalk which grows up into the air, surrounded by a few narrow leaves. The flowers of Onions are said to be in an umbel at the tip of the stem (though this umbel is not of the same origin as the true umbel of the Parsley and Primrose Families). In several species the flowers are replaced partly or wholly by small bulbs. The flowers, small as they are, have the same plan as those of a Lily.

Cernuum means "nodding" or "drooping," and refers to the manner in which the flowers of this species hang at the tip of the flower-stalk. The perianth varies from white to rose. At the base of the stalk one may find a cluster of bulbs attached to a short rootstock.

Allium cernuum grows over a wide range from New York to South Carolina and westward to British Columbia, Oregon and Arizona. The plant illustrated grew in the Ice River Valley, British Columbia, at an altitude of 4,000 feet.

Pl. 45. Wild Chives *Allium sibiricum*

The narrow bulbs of this species, up to an inch long, are clustered so that the leaves and flowers appear in a dense tuft. The leaves are awl-shaped and hollow, like those of the common cultivated Onion. The flowering stalk grows to 2 feet in height, and is densely flowered, but the stalks of the individual flowers are short. Species of this form are often cultivated for ornament in rock gardens.

Allium sibiricum is often classified as *Allium schoenoprasum* variety *sibiricum*. As its name indicates, it was first described from Siberia. It is distributed all around the world in the northern parts, in North America extending southward to New England, the Great Lakes region, Colorado and northern Oregon. The plant illustrated was found near Lake Louise in Alberta, at an altitude of 5,500 feet.

Pl. 46. Spanish Bayonet, Soapweed *Yucca navajoa*

The Yuccas of the southwestern United States are used by the Indians in many ways: the flowers, flower-stalks, fruits and seeds of various species are eaten, raw or cooked; the fibers of the leaves are used for making ropes, mats, baskets, cloth; the roots, known as amole, yield a detergent which is used in place of soap. The genus is a complex one and the species can be identified only by technical characters. Some of them are tree-like and known as Joshua Trees. *Yucca navajoa* is one of the smaller species, with an unbranched flower cluster from 2 to 3 feet high, bearing flowers nearly to the base. The perianth is about 2 inches long, its segments broad and concave. The stiff glossy leaves grow up to a foot long; the edges form many fine fibers.

The species has also been called *Yucca standleyi* and *Yucca baileyi*. It grows in Colorado, New Mexico,

Utah and Arizona. The plant sketched was found near Gallup, New Mexico.

Pl. 47. Bellwort *Uvularia perfoliata*

The common name refers to the hanging bell-shaped perianth, yellow and lily-like. The slender leafy stem grows from a short underground stem, from which spring also the thick fleshy roots. *Perfoliata* means "through the leaves," and refers to the manner in which the stem seems to have grown through each leaf blade.

This species of Bellwort grows in rich woods, flowering in spring before the trees are in leaf. It is found from Quebec to Florida and westward to Minnesota and Louisiana. The plant shown grew in Rock Creek Park, Washington, D. C.

Pl. 48. Blue Bead *Clintonia borealis*

The name Clintonia is from De Witt Clinton, the celebrated governor of New York from 1817 onward, to whom the genus was dedicated by Rafinesque. These are plants mostly of cool northern and mountain forests, with a few large lustrous leaves arising from an underground stem. The greenish-yellow lily-like flowers of *Clintonia borealis* grow in a cluster; they are succeeded by berries of a dark metallic blue.

The species grows from Labrador to North Carolina (along the mountains) and westward to Manitoba, Minnesota, Indiana and Tennessee. The specimen illustrated was found in Canandaigua, New York.

Pl. 49, 50. Queen Cup, Bride's Bonnet *Clintonia uniflora*

Queen Cup resembles the Blue Bead described above except that there is usually but one flower on a plant (sometimes there are 2). It grows in coniferous forests high in the mountains — from 3,500 to 6,000 feet up — from Alaska southward through the Cascade Mountains and the Sierra Nevada. The flowering plant illustrated came from near Field, British Columbia, at 4,500 feet; the fruiting plant grew on the Kootenay River, British Columbia, at 4,000 feet.

Pl. 51. False Solomon's Seal *Smilacina stellata*

Smilacina resembles *Polygonatum*, the Solomon's Seal, in general aspect, but the flowers of the former are clustered at the end of the stem, while those of the latter hang in twos and threes from the points where the leaves arise. The underground stem of *Smilacina* lacks the scaly "seals" which give *Polygonatum* its common name. This species of *Smilacina* has its small 6-parted flowers arranged singly along an unbranched flower stalk. In a related species common in the eastern states, the flower-stalk bears lateral branches, each of which carries clusters of flowers.

Smilacina stellata grows in most parts of North America where there are moist woods. The plant sketched came from near Lake Minnewonka, Alberta, at an altitude of 4,500 feet.

[18]

Pl. 52. Twisted-stalk *Streptopus amplexifolius*

The name Twisted-stalk is a translation of the generic name *Streptopus;* both refer to the sharp bend or twist near the middle of each flower-stalk. *Amplexifolius* means "embracing leaf," and alludes to the fact that the leaves clasp the stem. The stem forks; the leaves are glaucous (bluish-green) on the under side. The greenish-white perianth is rolled back. The fruit is a small egg-shaped red berry.

This species grows in moist woods from Greenland to North Carolina, westward to Alaska, Minnesota and New Mexico. The plant sketched was found near Hector, British Columbia, at an altitude of 5,000 feet.

Pl. 53. Western Twisted-stalk *Streptopus curvipes*

This species differs from the preceding in the purplish or reddish color of its perianth. The stem is usually unbranched and the entire plant is smaller.

Streptopus curvipes grows on shady slopes of the Coastal Ranges and the Cascade Mountains from Alaska to Oregon. The plant illustrated was collected near Glacier, British Columbia, at an altitude of 3,500 feet.

TRILLIUM, WAKE ROBIN *TRILLIUM*

The Trilliums have not only their flower parts in threes but their leaves also: there are 3 leaves just beneath the single flower. Furthermore, these leaves differ from most leaves of the Lily Family and related families in being net-veined instead of parallel-veined. The flowers also differ from most liliaceous flowers in having 3 green sepals contrasting with 3 colored petals. The stem arises from a short tuber underground. These plants are spring-flowering inhabitants of rich woods.

Pl. 54, 55. Purple Trillium *Trillium erectum*

The leaves are very broad with a short sharp point. The petals vary in color from brown-purple to pink, white or greenish. There are 3 distinct spreading stigmas. The scent of the flowers is unpleasant, for which reason it is sometimes called Stinking Benjamin. The pod is winged on the angles.

Plate 55 shows the white-flowered form of this species, sometimes classified as a distinct species under the name *Trillium album*.

Trillium erectum grows from Quebec to Georgia (in the mountains) and westward to Ontario and Tennessee. The specimen shown in Plate 54 was collected at Washington, D. C. The white-flowered form came from near Chestnut Hill, Massachusetts.

Pl. 56. Trillium *Trillium grandiflorum*

The petals of this species are unusually broad, at first white then turning rose-pink, or marked with green. The 3 stigmas are narrow but stand erect. The pod is almost globular, winged on the angles. There is a pink-flowered form in cultivation.

Trillium grandiflorum grows from Quebec to Georgia and westward to Minnesota and Missouri. The specimen illustrated came from Washington, D. C.

Pl. 57.   Painted Trillium
Trillium undulatum
This is the showiest of our Trilliums. The common name refers to the petals, with their red or purplish markings at the base. The leaves taper to their points. The pod is not winged, and rather broad.

Painted Trillium grows from Nova Scotia to Georgia (in the mountains) and westward to Wisconsin and Missouri. The specimen illustrated came from eastern Massachusetts.

Pl. 58.   Toadshade   *Trillium sessile*
Sessile means, literally "sitting," hence "without a stalk"; the flower grows from the tip of the stem at the same point as the 3 leaves and lacks a stalk of its own. The petals are narrow and in the common form of the species they are colored reddish-brown; other forms, like that shown in the painting, have greenish petals. The leaves are usually marked with brown spots. The plant is rather smaller than the other species here illustrated.

A related species, *Trillium recurvatum,* has petals narrowed at the base to a short claw; the leaves also have short stalks.

Trillium sessile grows from Pennsylvania to Virginia and westward to Missouri and Arkansas. The plants illustrated were found on Plummer's Island in the Potomac River near Washington, D. C.

Pl. 59.   Giant Trillium
Trillium chloropetalum
The Giant Trillium grows to a height of nearly 2 feet. It has almost round leaves, which are usually mottled. The flower is sessile like that of *Trillium sessile.* The petals are maroon or greenish-yellow or even white. The first form discovered, from which the species was named, was the greenish-flowered form; *chloropetalum* means "with green petals." The fruit is conspicuously winged.

Giant Trillium ranges from Washington to California. The specimen from which the painting was made was cultivated in Boston, Massachusetts.

Amaryllis family. Amaryllidaceae

Pl. 60.   Atamasco Lily
Zephyranthes atamasco
In spite of the common name, this species is not a member of the Lily Family, but is placed in the family which contains the Amaryllis, Agave, and Narcissus. The difference is that these plants have an inferior ovary — the ovary is immersed in the tissues of the flower stalk and base of the flower and inseparable from them. Otherwise this plant is lily-like in appearance and in the plan of the flower.

Atamasco (an Indian name) Lily grows from Pennsylvania to Florida. The plant used for illustration was found at Yemassee, South Carolina.

Pl. 61.   Spider Lily   *Hymenocallis rotata*
The Spider Lily grows in clumps from bulbs usually along sandy shores and at times submerged. The leaves are stiff, erect, sword-like. The leafless flower-stalk bears several flowers. The genus is known by the delicate veil or membrane which connects the stalks of the stamens; a funnel-shaped structure, often toothed, which somewhat recalls the crown of the Daffodil and Narcissus (also in this family). This species is known also by its extremely narrow perianth parts.

The identity of the species is controversial, and various names have been applied to it. It is perhaps the same as *Hymenocallis caribaea,* which Small called *Hymenocallis keyensis.*

The Spider Lily grows in southern Florida and along the coastal plain to South Carolina. The plant illustrated was collected on Loggerhead Key in the Dry Tortugas, Florida.

Pl. 62.   Star Grass   *Hypoxis hirsuta*
The yellow perianth marks this plant as not a true grass, in spite of its narrow leaves. The leaves overtop the flower-stalk, which bears usually several small 6-parted flowers with inferior ovaries (usually only one in bloom at a time). The perianth is greenish outside and hairy.

Star Grass grows in meadows and open woodlands from Maine to Florida and westward to Manitoba, Kansas and Texas.

Iris family. Iridaceae

The Iris Family includes several kinds of plants that at first sight do not suggest the Iris: Gladiolus, Freesia, Sisyrinchium. Some members of the family have irregular flowers, in which the upper parts differ from the lower in shape, size, and sometimes color; others, like the Iris itself and Blue-eyed Grass, have a regular perianth, radially symmetrical. The Iris Family resembles the Amaryllis Family in having an inferior ovary; it differs from it in having 3 stamens instead of 6.

Pl. 63.   Blue-eyed Grass
Sisyrinchium angustifolium
Like Star Grass, this plant owes its English name to it narrow grass-like leaves; members of the Grass Family do not have a colored perianth. The leaves of Blue-eyed Grass are like those of Iris in arrangement. Two small membranous scales which are folded

around the bases of the flower-stalks in this genus form a spathe (compare the Araceae, in which family the spathe consists of one leaf). The inferior ovary becomes a small brown globular pod.

Sisyrinchium angustifolium grows in fields and wet sandy soil from Newfoundland to Virginia, westward to British Columbia, and southward in the Rocky Mountains. The plants illustrated were found in the valley of the Ghost River near Banff, Alberta, at an altitude of 4,000 feet.

IRIS *IRIS*

The flowers of Iris are well known and sufficiently identify the genus. The 6-parted perianth consists of 3 outer, erect parts: the standards; and 3 inner, reflexed parts: the falls; both of these sets have a wide variety of colors and markings. There are 3 stamens, projecting over the 3 falls. And the 3 branches of the style resemble petals in texture and color; they extend over the stamens, carrying the stigmas on their lower surface. The ovary, as in all members of the family, is inferior.

The leaves, which arise from an underground stem or tuber, are curiously folded, each embracing the next younger. Linnaeus described this arrangement fancifully as equitant, i.e., after the manner of a rider bestriding a horse. This peculiar feature is found also in other members of the family.

Pl. 64. Large Blue Flag *Iris versicolor*

The Large Blue Flag has standards considerably longer than the falls. The falls lack the crest or beard which are found in other species (e.g., the common garden Bearded Iris).

Iris versicolor grows in wet places from Labrador and Newfoundland to Virginia and westward to Manitoba and Minnesota. The plant illustrated was found near Washington, D. C.

Pl. 65. Dwarf Iris *Iris verna*

This Iris is recognized by its low stature (only 6 inches high) and grass-like leaves. The falls and standards are about equal in length. There is no crest or beard on the falls. The pod is blunt on the angles.

Dwarf Iris is found on wooded hillsides from Pennsylvania to Florida and westward to Kentucky and Mississippi, mostly on sandy soil. The painting was made near Beaufort, South Carolina.

Pl. 66. Crested Dwarf Iris *Iris cristata*

The crest which gives this Iris its name is the crinkled projection on the upper side of the falls. The flowers are sweet-smelling. The leaves are broader, less grass-like, than those of *Iris verna*. The pod is sharply triangular in section.

Iris cristata grows in rich woods from Maryland to Georgia and westward to Indiana and Missouri. The plants shown in the painting were found on Plummer's Island in the Potomac River near Washington, D. C.

Orchid family. Orchidaceae

The Orchids are usually associated with wealth and luxury; yet many species grow wild in our fields and forests. The largest and most gorgeous kinds are tropical; but even the smallest and least conspicuous share the complex flower structure which characterizes the family. The flower has 3 sepals and 3 petals. Of the petals, one, usually the lowermost, is different from the others in size, shape or color — or all three; this is called the lip. There is a single stamen in most of our orchids; 2 in the Lady's-slipper; and the stamen or stamens are united with the style and stigma to form a complex structure called the column, which occupies the center of the flower. At the summit of the column the pollen is more or less exposed, cohering in small masses called pollinia, and variously provided with an elaborate mechanism which affixes it to the bodies of visiting insects. Below the pollen is the large stigmatic surface. The ovary is inferior, and has 1 or 3 chambers. The ovary, with the surrounding tissues of the stem in which it is immersed, becomes a pod, usually 3-angled. The seeds are minute and very numerous.

Most of the tropical Orchids grow as epiphytes — not parasites — upon the trunks of trees. Epiphytes merely use other plants as supports, having themselves no direct connection with the ground; parasites, like Dodder and Mistletoe, obtain their nourishment from the host plant. Many of the epiphytic species bear pseudobulbs — large swollen branches which are reservoirs of food and water; their aerial roots are able to take water from the humid air. Our species often grow in boggy or acid soil, rich in organic matter, where their roots are associated with certain fungi — on which they are perhaps parasitic or partly so. Such complex relationships make it extremely difficult to transplant Orchids and cultivate them in ordinary gardens.

LADY'S-SLIPPER *CYPRIPEDIUM*

The name Lady's-slipper or Moccasin-flower refers to the large lip. Pollination is effected by bees and other insects, which enter the lip by the opening in its upper side and feed on the nectar inside; to escape they must crawl out past the column, taking with them some of the sticky pollen-masses; these may come in contact with the stigma of the next flower visited.

In most species of this genus the 2 lower sepals are united so that there appear to be only 2 in all.

Pl. 67. Ram's-head Lady's-slipper
Cypripedium arietinum

This is the only North American Lady's-slipper in which the 3 sepals are all distinct. The sepals and the lateral petals are greenish-brown; the lip is streaked white and red. The lip, only half an inch long, has a conical projection below. The species is easily distinguished also by its slender stature and narrow, lance-shaped leaves. A single flower grows at the summit of the stem.

Ram's-head Lady's-slipper grows from Quebec to New York and westward to Manitoba, Wisconsin and Illinois. It occurs also in China. The plant illustrated grew in Chittenden County, Vermont.

Pl. 68. Yellow Lady's-slipper
Cypripedium calceolus

This orchid has a leafy stem up to 2 feet tall; the leaves, which are broad and embrace the stem, are strongly veined lengthwise, dark green and downy. There are 1 or 2 flowers at the summit of the stem. The twisted sepals and lateral petals vary from greenish-yellow to brownish-purple, the lip from cream-colored to golden yellow.

Cypripedium calceolus grows from Quebec and Newfoundland to Georgia and westward to the Yukon, British Columbia, Washington, Oregon, Utah and Arizona, as well as in Europe and Asia. As would be expected from such a wide distribution, it exists in a number of varieties, which have often been classified as distinct species. The plant illustrated was collected in North Carolina; it belongs to the variety *parviflorum.*

Pl. 69. Showy Lady's-slipper
Cypripedium reginae

The Showy Lady's-slipper is one of the most gorgeous of our species. The lip is an inch or more long, white, and usually suffused with pink and decorated with purplish streaks. The sepals and lateral petals are white. There may be from 1 to 3 flowers at the summit of the leafy stem. The short coarse hairs of stem and leaves may cause an irritation of the skin similar to that caused by Poison Ivy.

Cypripedium reginae grows from Newfoundland to North Carolina and westward to Saskatchewan, North Dakota, Iowa, Missouri and Tennessee; also in China. The plant shown in the painting was collected in Lenox, Massachusetts.

Pl. 70. Mountain Lady's-slipper
Cypripedium montanum

This species has a leafy stem which grows to a height of 2 feet and more. The long sepals are twisted; they and the petals vary from dark green to brownish-purple. The lip is white with pink or purplish lines.

Mountain Lady's-slipper occurs from Montana and Wyoming westward to Alaska, British Columbia, Washington, Oregon and California. The painting was made near Radium Hot Springs, British Columbia.

Pl. 71, 72. Pink Moccasin-flower
Cypripedium acaule

The leaves of this Mocassin-flower spring directly from the ground, instead of being borne on a visible stem (*acaule* means "stemless"); the true stem is underground. There are 2 leaves, deep green and glossy. The lip is cleft along the upper side, with the edges inrolled and in contact (instead of provided with a distinct small opening like the lips of the other species). In the commoner form shown in Plate 71, the lip is pink; in other forms, one of which is illustrated in Plate 72, it varies from pale pink to cream-colored and even pure white.

Cypripedium acaule is found from Newfoundland to Georgia and westward to Alberta, Indiana, Kentucky and Alabama. The specimens illustrated grew near Washington, D. C.

Pl. 73. Showy Orchis   Orchis spectabilis

The Showy Orchis forms but 2 leaves, broad and glossy and sheathing the base of the flowering stem. The flowers rarely rise to a height of more than a foot above the ground. The sepals and lateral petals come together over the column to form a sort of hood, usually rose-pink or lilac in color, sometimes even purple, rarely almost white. The lip is white, and extends backward beside the flower-stalk in a tubular spur, in which nectar collects.

It is found from New Brunswick and Quebec to Georgia and westward to Minnesota, Nebraska, Kansas and Arkansas. The painting was made near Washington, D. C.

Pl. 74. Round-leaved Orchis
Orchis rotundifolia

As the painting shows, the plant forms a single leaf close to the ground. The flowering stem grows to a height of about a foot, bearing as many as 16 flowers. Like the preceding species, the lateral petals and sepals, which vary from white to pink or mauve, form a hood over the column. The lip is white, spotted with magenta-pink or purplish, and is 3-lobed.

Charles Darwin conducted his celebrated experiments upon pollination with European species of this genus.

The Round-leaved Orchis grows from Greenland to New York and westward to Alaska, British Columbia and Wyoming. The plants shown were found near Field, British Columbia, at an altitude of 3,800 feet.

REIN-ORCHIS, FRINGED ORCHIS
HABENARIA

Habenaria is a large genus of about 500 species which grow in woodlands, meadows and swamps all over the world; at least 39 species occur in North America. There are usually many small flowers closely arranged on one flowering stem. The uppermost sepal forms a hood over the column; the 2 lateral petals adhere to this; the other sepals extend outward. The lip is prolonged backward into a hollow spur, in which nectar collects.

Pl. 75. Orange-plume   Habenaria ciliaris

The stem of this species may grow to a height of more than 3 feet; it bears a number of lance-shaped, rather rigid leaves. The lip is copiously fringed to a length of nearly half an inch (*ciliaris* means "provided

[21]

with cilia" or eyelashes, and refers to this fringe).

Orange-plume is found from Ontario to Florida and westward to Wisconsin, Missouri and Texas. The plant illustrated grew near Bridgeport, Connecticut.

Pl. 76. Ragged Orchid *Habenaria lacera*

The Ragged Orchid derives its name from the lip, which is deeply 3-lobed with the lobes again divided and torn (*lacera*) into a ragged fringe of long hair-like divisions. The flowers vary in color from yellowish-green to whitish or even light bronze. The flowering stem rises to a height of 2 feet or more; it bears a number of narrow rigid leaves.

Habenaria lacera occurs from Newfoundland to Georgia and westward to Manitoba, Missouri, Oklahoma and Texas. The specimen illustrated was found near Washington, D. C.

Pl. 77. Purple Fringed Orchis
Habenaria psycodes

This species has a stem sometimes over 3 feet high, which bears several large sheathing leaves. The flowers vary in color from almost white to pinkish or lavender. The lip is deeply cleft in 3 parts, the lateral divisions themselves cleft, and all the margin deeply fringed (*psycodes* means "butterfly-like"). The flowers vary greatly also in size; plants with large flowers (the lip ¾ inch long) have sometimes been classified as a variety or even as a distinct species, *Habenaria grandiflora*.

Purple Fringed Orchis grows from Newfoundland to Georgia and westward to Minnesota, Iowa and Kentucky. The painting was made on Mount Desert Island, Maine.

Pl. 78. One-leaved Rein-orchis
Habenaria obtusata

The plant has usually but one leaf, at the base of the stem. The stem grows only about a foot high. The flowers are small and greenish. The sepals are broader than the petals. The lip is narrow, with a curved spur about as long as the lip proper.

Habenaria obtusata is found in bogs and wet soil often at high altitudes (11,500 feet in Colorado), from Labrador to New York and westward to Alaska, Minnesota and Utah. The plant illustrated grew near Banff, Alberta, at an altitude of 4,000 feet.

Pl. 79. Heart-leaved Twayblade
Listera cordata

This inconspicuous delicate plant scarcely suggests an orchid at first sight. It is only 10 inches high or less. The name Twayblade refers to the 2 leaves which grow on the stem. *Cordata* alludes to their heart-shaped outline. There are 2 color-forms: in the west, plants are found with greenish flowers, while the usual form throughout the range of the species has dark purplish flowers. The flowers have a long narrow lip cut halfway to the base or more into two segments, and bearing a transverse tooth on each side near the base.

Listera cordata grows from Greenland to North Carolina (in the mountains) and westward to Alaska and California. The plants used for illustration were collected in Yoho Pass near Field, British Columbia, at an altitude of 3,800 feet.

Pl. 80. Rosebud Orchid *Cleistes divaricata*

The Rosebud Orchid has only one leaf, about halfway up the stem. The stem grows to a height of 2 feet or more. The sepals extend out ("divaricately") and are rolled back at the tip. The 3 petals grow close together around the column, simulating a long rosebud; the lip has a rather fleshy crest down its midline.

Cleistes divaricata is rather rare; it is found from New Jersey to Florida and westward to Kentucky and Texas. The plant illustrated came from Beaufort, South Carolina.

Pl. 81. Rose Pogonia
Pogonia ophioglossoides

This graceful orchid usually has but one leaf and one flower; but, as in the painting, some plants (especially those of the south) have 2 or 3 flowers, with a corresponding number of leaves. The stem grows as much as 2 feet high. The flowers vary in color from white to rose, all the segments of the perianth being of much the same shade. The lip is abundantly fringed, and bears a beard of yellowish hairs near its center. The flowers are said to have the fragrance of fresh raspberries.

Rose Pogonia is fairly common in bogs from Newfoundland and Quebec to Florida and westward to Minnesota, Missouri and Texas. The plants shown were found near Tuckerton, New Jersey.

Pl. 82. Arethusa *Arethusa bulbosa*

Arethusa, named after the nymph of classical story, forms a single flower on a leafless stalk rising only about a foot from the ground. The one leaf, narrow and grass-like, develops after flowering. The sepals and lateral petals are of the same color, usually pink or pinkish-purple, sometimes bluish or white. The lip is somewhat frilled at the end and bearded with fleshy yellow hairs with purple tips. The flower is fragrant.

Arethusa grows in bogs, wet meadows and swamps from Newfoundland and Quebec to North Carolina and westward to Minnesota and Wisconsin. The plant sketched was found near Washington, D. C., where the species is extremely rare.

Pl. 83. Grass-pink *Calopogon pulchellus*

The Grass-pink superficially resembles Pogonia, but is readily distinguished by having the lip uppermost instead of in the more usual position. This is actually the position in which we would expect to find the lip, for it is really the upper petal in all orchids; but in most species the stalk twists (and this is easily seen in the twisting of its lengthwise ribs) so that the entire flower is inverted. Grass-pink grows to a height of 4 feet or more. There is usually a single narrow leaf at the base of the stem; but some northern plants have a pair. The lip is conspicuously bearded with fleshy purple and orange hairs.

Grass-pink occurs from Newfoundland and Quebec to Florida and westward to Minnesota, Missouri and Texas; also in Cuba and the Bahama Islands. The specimen illustrated grew near Tuckerton, New Jersey.

LADIES' TRESSES   *SPIRANTHES*

The genus *Spiranthes* contains some 300 species of orchids. They bear a flowering stem on which the small flowers are closely packed usually in a spiral (whence the name). The flowers are usually white or greenish, in some species red or orange or lavender. The upper sepal adheres to the lateral petals to form a small hood over the column. The genus is known in tropical Asia, Australia and New Zealand as well as in Europe and North and South America.

Pl. 84. Hooded Ladies' Tresses
Spiranthes romanzoffiana
This is one of the larger species, growing sometimes 2 feet tall. The leaves are mostly basal, rather grass-like. The flower-stalk bears many rather large flowers, the sepals and lateral petals forming a hood over the column, the lip half an inch long, white and sweet-scented.

Hooded Ladies' Tresses grow in swampy land from Newfoundland and Labrador to New York and westward to Alaska and California; also in Ireland. The species extends to high elevations in the mountains (10,000 feet in the western states). The plants sketched come from the Siffleur River Valley in Alberta, at an altitude of 4,500 feet.

Pl. 85. Nodding Ladies' Tresses
Spiranthes cernua
Slender Ladies' Tresses
Spiranthes gracilis
These 2 species are readily distinguished by the size of their flowers. In the first, the flowers nod or droop on their stalks (*cernua* means "nodding"). The flowering stem may reach a height of nearly 2 feet. The leaves are narrow, mostly situated at the base of the flowering stem, and soon disappear. The lip is nearly half an inch long, white, fragrant, ruffled at the edge. The flowers of *Spiranthes gracilis* are very small—the lip only ¼ inch long or less — and the spike of flowers is therefore very slim (*gracilis* means "slender"). The lip is fringed and has a green stripe in the center. The leaves are at the base and soon wither.

Both species have about the same range, from Nova Scotia and Quebec to Florida and westward to the Dakotas, Kansas and New Mexico. *Spiranthes cernua* is found usually in wet soil or bogs, *Spiranthes gracilis* in dry soil. Both the plants illustrated were collected near Mt. Kisco, New York.

Pl. 86. Rattlesnake Plantain
Goodyera oblongifolia
Rattlesnake Plantain is characterized by its dark green leaves which are usually marked with a pattern of whitish lines (suggesting snake skin and giving the plant its common name). The flower-spike somewhat resembles that of Ladies' Tresses. The flowers are small and greenish; the lateral petals with the upper sepal form a hood over the column and lip. The lip is short and not cut or lobed.

This species of *Goodyera* grows from Nova Scotia to Maine and westward to Alaska and California. The leaves vary in the degree to which they are marked with white. In another species, found in the Atlantic states, the variegation is more prominent. The plant shown in the illustration was found near Glacier, British Columbia, at an altitude of 3,000 feet.

Pl. 87. Calypso, Cytherea
Calypso bulbosa
Like Arethusa, this beautiful orchid was named after one of the nymphs of classical legend. It grows from a corm, an underground tuber-like stem. Only one leaf is formed, which appears late in the season and lasts through the winter; it is broad and long-stalked. Only one flower also is formed, hanging from the end of a stalk about 8 inches tall. The lateral petals and the sepals are alike in color. The column is broad and conspicuous. The brightly colored lip suggests one of the Lady's-slippers, to which, however, this species is not related.

Calypso grows in deep woods from Labrador to New York and westward to Washington, Oregon and California; also in Europe and Asia. The painting was made in Glacier National Park, Montana.

Pl. 88. Twayblade   *Liparis liliifolia*
The plant grows only 10 inches tall, but has 2 conspicuous broad and glossy, strongly veined leaves. These, with the flowering stem, arise from a sort of bulb-like stem underground. The flower cluster is open — that is, the flowers are not crowded together. Sepals and lateral petals are very narrow, ⅛ inch or less in width, and about ½ inch long. The lip is about 2/5 inch wide, of a brownish-mauve or purplish color, and sharply bent down.

Twayblade grows rarely in northern New England, and is found more often in open woods from Virginia to Georgia and westward to Minnesota, Missouri and Alabama; also in China. The plant illustrated was found on High Island in the Potomac River near Washington, D. C.

Pl. 89. Butterfly Orchid
Epidendrum tampense
The genus *Epidendrum* is mostly tropical; there are about 800 species scattered through Mexico, Central and South America and the West Indies. Most of the species grow attached to trees (*Epidendrum* is from two Greek words meaning "upon a tree"). Several species grow in Florida. The yellowish sepals and

lateral petals are alike in color, and contrast with the pink-striped lip, which is 3-lobed.

This is the most abundant epiphytic orchid in Florida. It occurs also in Cuba and the Bahama Islands.

Pl. 90.   Night-smelling Epidendrum
Epidendrum nocturnum

In form the flower of *Epidendrum nocturnum* resembles that of *Epidendrum tampense,* but its perianth consists of much narrower parts. The lip is curiously 3-lobed. The flowers are especially fragrant at night.

The Night-smelling Epidendrum grows on various trees in the hammocks of southern Florida; also in Mexico, Central America, northern South America and the West Indies. The plant shown in the painting came from Coot's Bay, Florida.

Pl. 91.   Bee-swarm or Cowhorn Orchid
Cyrtopodium punctatum

The Bee-swarm Orchid answers the popular concept of an orchid better than most North American species of the family. It is a large epiphytic species, often over 3 feet tall. The leaves and flower stalks grow from pseudobulbs which are sometimes over a foot long (the "cowhorns"). The lateral petals and the sepals are much alike in form and color. The lip is joined with the base of the column; it is 3-lobed and thick and warty in the middle.

The Bee-swarm Orchid is found on tree trunks or rotten logs in hammocks and cypress swamps of southern Florida; also in Mexico, Central and South America, and the West Indies. It has long been known in cultivation. The plant shown in the painting was collected at Coot's Bay, Florida.

Willow family. Salicaceae

Pl. 92.   Pussy Willow   *Salix discolor*

The genus *Salix* includes some 300 species which grow mostly in the north temperate zone, frequently along streams or in swamps. More than 100 are found in North America. The species are often difficult to distinguish, and matters are complicated by the fact that many species hybridize in nature. Staminate and pistillate flowers are borne on different plants, in pendent clusters known as catkins. They have no perianth. Each staminate flower consists only of a few stamens (from 1 to 7); each pistillate flower consists of a single pistil. A small scale grows underneath each flower; there is also a small gland (or sometimes 2) at the base of stamens or pistil. In some species the catkins appear before the leaves, in others at the same time. The gray silky hairs that appear early in spring on branches of Pussy Willow are attached to the scales of the catkins. As they lengthen, the 2 stamens or the single pistil of each flower become evident.

Pussy Willow grows from Newfoundland to Delaware and westward to British Columbia and Missouri. The illustration was made from a plant growing in Washington, D. C.

Pl. 93.   Drummond's Willow
Salix drummondiana

This is a species of the high mountains. The leaves are whitened on the under surface with fine curled hairs. There are 2 stamens in each staminate flower. The illustration shows the capsules open and liberating the seeds; the fine hairs grow from the seed-coats, enabling the wind to carry the seeds long distances.

Drummond's Willow grows in the Rocky Mountains in Alberta and British Columbia. The painting was made on Sheep Creek, Alberta, at an elevation of 6,000 feet.

Pl. 94.   Snow Willow   *Salix nivalis*

This diminutive plant, only one or 2 inches high, would never be recognized as a willow, not even as a woody plant, by most persons finding it. The leaf blades are oval, or round, and smooth, rather bluish-green on the under side. The small catkins, brownish or orange in color, terminate the short stems.

Snow Willow grows at high altitudes from Montana to British Columbia and Washington. The sketch was made at Bow Lake, Alberta, at an altitude of 7,000 feet.

Birch family. Betulaceae

Pl. 95.   Smooth Alder   *Alnus rugosa*

The flowers of Alders, like those of Willows, are borne in catkins; staminate and pistillate flowers are in different catkins but on the same plant. The flowers lack petals but sepals are present. Each of the scales of the staminate catkin is associated with 3 flowers; each scale of the pistillate catkin with 2. There are 4 stamens in each staminate flower, a single pistil in each pistillate flower. Smooth Alder has rather blunt leaves, the edges of which are cut into fine teeth which are themselves toothed; the veins are rather prominent on the under side (*rugosa* means "wrinkled") and sometimes downy. The painting shows the staminate cones, which open and shed the pollen in spring before the leaves appear. The bark yields a yellow dye.

Smooth Alder grows usually in swamps and along streams from Nova Scotia to Maryland and westward to Minnesota and Indiana; also in Europe and Asia.

Pl. 96.   Mountain Alder   *Alnus sinuata*

The pistillate catkins of Alder, as they mature and form their small nuts, become woody cones. The illustration of Mountain Alder shows the condition in the autumn, when the pistillate cones of the previous spring are mature and woody, and the staminate cones which will open the following spring are already present. This is a shrub with sharp leaves, round at the base, smooth, sharply double-toothed and cut.

The staminate catkins may be 3 inches long; the pistillate catkins are less than an inch long in the spring when pollination occurs.

Mountain Alder grows along streams from Wyoming to British Columbia and southward in the Cascade Mountains to Oregon. The illustration was made near Glacier, British Columbia, at an altitude of 3,500 feet.

Sandalwood family.
Santalaceae

Pl. 97. Bastard Toad-flax *Comandra livida*
Very few members of the Sandalwood Family grow in North America. This species is a perennial herb growing from an underground stem, about a foot high. The flowers lack petals; they have 5 stamens which arise between the lobes of a fleshy disc which lines the inside of the flower. The ovary is about half inferior. The fruit is small, succulent, red, crowned by the remains of the sepals. It grows in bogs and wet woods, where, like other members of the genus, it is probably parasitic on the roots of other plants.

Comandra livida is found from Labrador to northern New England and westward to Alaska and Washington. The specimen illustrated came from Glacier Lake in Alberta, at an altitude of 6,000 feet.

Mistletoe family.
Loranthaceae

Pl. 98. Mistletoe *Phoradendron flavescens*
Mistletoe is a true parasite, which sends suckers into the host tree and obtains food from it. Its greenish flowers have sepals but no petals. The stamens and pistils are found on different plants. The staminate flower has its sepals joined into a 3-lobed cup, and 3 stamens. The ovary is inferior and becomes the white berry.

This is not the common mistletoe of Europe, which is *Viscum album;* but both are placed in the same family. There are about 100 species of *Phoradendron,* all American and mostly tropical. Another large genus in this family is *Loranthus,* whose flowers are sometimes very showy.

Mistletoe grows from New Jersey to Florida and westward to Missouri and New Mexico. The specimen illustrated grew in Virginia.

Birthwort family.
Aristolochiaceae

Pl. 99. Wild Ginger *Asarum canadense*
This plant, whose leaves rise only about 6 inches from the ground, has a stem which grows just beneath the surface; this stem has a pungent odor when broken, from which the common name is derived. The small flowers grow at the base of the leaves. The cup formed by the sepals is 3-lobed; there are no petals; there are 12 stamens and an inferior ovary containing 6 chambers and bearing a 6-lobed stigma. The species has been divided by some botanists into several; by others these are considered varieties of one species. The plant shown is apparently variety *ambiguum.*

Wild Ginger grows in woods from New Brunswick and Quebec to North Carolina and westward to Minnesota, Arkansas and Alabama. The illustration was made from a plant on Plummer's Island in the Potomac River near Washington, D. C.

Goosefoot family.
Chenopodiaceae

Pl. 100. Strawberry Blite
              Chenopodium capitatum
Many species of *Chenopodium* are weeds in gardens; the commonest is generally known as Lamb's Quarters. The flowers in this genus are small and greenish, with sepals but no petals, usually 5 stamens and an ovary bearing 2 or 3 styles. Some species are eaten as greens. Spinach and Beet are also members of the family. Strawberry Blite is easily known by the enlarged sepals which become fleshy and red as the fruit within them develops. The fruit itself is a small bladder containing a single seed.

Strawberry Blite grows in open places from Quebec to New Jersey westward to Alaska, and southward in the Rocky Mountains. The plant shown was found in Bow Valley, Alberta, at an altitude of 4,000 feet.

Pink family.
Caryophyllaceae

Pl. 101. Nodding Campion *Lychnis apetala*
This curious alpine plant has a much inflated sac formed from the joined sepals, which lasts until the fruit is formed within it. In spite of the name (*apetala* means "without petals") petals are present, but they

are small and scarcely protrude from the sepal tube.

Nodding Campion is found from Greenland to Alaska and southward to Labrador, Montana, Colorado and Utah; also in Europe and Asia. The painting was made from a plant near Lake McArthur, British Columbia, at an altitude of 7,000 feet.

Pl. 102.   Wild Pink   *Silene caroliniana*

The Pinks bear a superficial resemblance to Phlox. *Silene* has 5 sepals joined into a tube, 5 petals all separate, 10 stamens, and an ovary bearing usually 3 styles. The fruit is a small pod or capsule bearing many small seeds attached to a short column which arises from the base, and opens by splitting into 6 teeth. *Silene caroliniana* has a perennial root, from which grows the flowering stem about 8 inches tall. As in many species of this genus, the stems are sticky. The petals vary from white to dark pink.

The Wild Pink grows in rocky places from New Hampshire to South Carolina and westward to Missouri and Alabama. The plant shown was found near Washington, D. C.

Pl. 103.   Moss Campion   *Silene acaulis*

This is an alpine species, growing in dense tussocks which rise only a few inches from the ground. Each stem is terminated by a single flower. The petals are pink, lilac or white. The capsule is partly divided into three chambers. The plant somewhat resembles the well-known Moss Pink, which is a species of Phlox, but differs in having the petals not united.

Moss Campion grows in the Arctic regions and southward to Nova Scotia, New Hampshire and Alaska and in the mountains to Arizona and Washington; also in Europe and Asia. The plant shown in the painting grew near Lake Louise in Alberta, at an altitude of 7,500 feet.

Purslane family. Portulacaceae

Pl. 104.   Spring Beauty
Claytonia virginica

This early-flowering plant is well known, though its common name is shared with several other quite different species. Typically, Spring Beauty has a single pair of opposite leaves; the flower has 2 sepals and 5 petals, within which are 5 stamens and an ovary crowned by a 3-cleft style. Each pinkish flower blooms for a day, after which it bends to one side and a lateral flower starts from below it and pushes up to bloom in its turn. The plant grows from a small bulb-like stem.

Spring Beauty grows in woods and openings from Nova Scotia to Georgia and westward to Montana and Texas. It is often found in lawns. The painting was made at Washington, D. C.

Pl. 105.   Naiad Spring Beauty
Montia parvifolia

Montia is a close relative of *Claytonia*. Its leaves are partly paired but many are scattered singly along the stems. The flowers are like those of Spring Beauty, but there are 3 distinct styles. The plant grows from an underground stem.

Naiad Spring Beauty occurs on the banks of streams from Alaska to California. The plant shown in the painting was found near Glacier House in the Selkirk Mountains of British Columbia, at an altitude of 3,500 feet.

Water-lily family. Nymphaeaceae

Pl. 106.   Water-lily   *Nymphaea odorata*

The stem of the Water-lily grows on the bottom of a pool or slow stream, rooting in the mud. The long leaf-stalks and the flower-stalks are attached to this underwater stem; they are pierced by channels filled with gases which thus circulate beneath the surface of the water. There are 4 sepals and many petals; the latter pass gradually into stamens through intermediate bodies (illustrating the commonly held botanical theory that petals are transformed stamens). The pistil is large and composed of many segments; each segment bears a stigma on its summit and all the stigmas radiate like the spokes of a wheel from a projection in the center. The flowers are fragrant.

Nymphaea odorata grows from Newfoundland to Florida and westward to Manitoba, Minnesota and Louisiana; also in Mexico, the West Indies and South America. The plant illustrated was found near Washington, D. C.

Pl. 107.   Yellow Pond-lily   *Nuphar advena*

The Yellow Pond-lily grows in much the same situations as the Water-lily described above. The flowers have 5 or more large concave yellow sepals; the numerous petals resemble the stamens and are not conspicuous. The ovary and stigmas are much like those of *Nymphaea*.

Nuphar advena is found from Maine to Florida and westward to Nebraska and Texas. The plant illustrated grew near Washington, D. C.

Buttercup family. Ranunculaceae

The Buttercup Family contains a large number of familiar plants — Buttercup, Anemone, Peony, Clematis, Columbine, Larkspur, and others. They are all herbaceous genera (i.e., not woody). The flower parts are mostly numerous and all separate. This applies even to the pistils, which are simple, each 1-chambered, each developing separately into a pod, a berry or a small nut-like 1-seeded fruit. Petals may be lacking and the sepals brightly colored instead. The family is relatively primitive, for the earliest flowering plants are thought to have had numerous distinct parts.

Pl. 108. Globe-flower *Trollius laxus*

The stem of this *Trollius* grows a foot or more high. The stalkless leaves are divided into toothed segments which radiate from the point of attachment to the stem. The flower consists of several yellow or whitish sepals (resembling petals, which are absent) and numerous stamens and pistils. The pistils become pods, each containing a number of seeds.

Trollius laxus grows in wet meadows and swamps from New Hampshire to Delaware and westward to British Columbia and Utah. The illustration was made from a plant growing in the alpine meadows of Mt. Assiniboine, Alberta, at an altitude of 6,500 feet.

Pl. 109. Heart-leaved Caltha
Caltha leptosepala

The leaves of *Caltha leptosepala* are longer than broad, contrasting with those of the following species. The sepals are bluish-white instead of yellow. Otherwise the 2 species are much alike.

Heart-leaved Caltha grows in bogs and alpine meadows high in the mountains from Montana to Alaska and southward to Oregon. The painting was made from plants collected near Mt. Assiniboine in Alberta, at an altitude of 5,000 feet.

Pl. 110. Marsh Marigold, Cowslip
Caltha palustris

Several American flowers are miscalled Cowslip (see Pl. 314), a name which properly belongs to a well-known English flower of the genus *Primula*. True Marigold belongs to still another family, the Compositae (see p. 59). The Marsh Marigold has a flower composed of 5 or more petal-like sepals; true petals are lacking. The pistils become many-seeded pods. The broad smooth leaves are sometimes boiled and eaten in early spring.

Caltha palustris grows in wet meadows and swamps, often in standing water, all across North America from Labrador to Alaska and southward to South Carolina, Tennessee and Nebraska. The plant sketched was collected near Chestnut Hill, Massachusetts.

Pl. 111. Columbine *Aquilegia canadensis*

The adjective *canadensis,* Canadian, was given to many species when Canada extended from the St. Lawrence to New Orleans and westward. This Columbine has a similarly wide range. The 5 red petals are prolonged backward into tubular spurs in which nectar is formed. The sepals are yellowish. There are many stamens, and a few pistils which become many-seeded pods. Each leaf is composed of distinct segments which are themselves cut and the ultimate parts are lobed.

Columbine grows usually on rocky ledges in woodlands from Newfoundland and Quebec to Saskatchewan and southward to Florida and Texas. The painting was made from plants found near Washington, D. C.

Pl. 112. Yellow Columbine
Aquilegia flavescens

This western Columbine grows to a height of more than 2 feet. The leaves are less divided than those of the preceding species. The flowers may be pure light yellow or (as in the painting) flushed with red. In the center of the tuft of stamens the ends of the styles are visible.

Yellow Columbine grows in open woods from Wyoming to British Columbia and southward to Utah and Oregon. The plant illustrated was collected in the Ptarmigan Valley near Lake Louise, Alberta, at an altitude of 6,000 feet.

Pl. 113. Shortspur Columbine
Aquilegia brevistyla

In the eastern United States only two species of *Aquilegia* are known; and one of these was introduced from Europe. In the mountain states there are many species, with flowers of many hues. The state flower of Colorado is a blue Columbine, *Aquilegia coerulea.*

The sepals of *Aquilegia brevistyla* are blue or lavender, the petals light yellow. The spurs are only about ¼ inch long.

Shortspur Columbine grows in meadows and open woods from Minnesota westward through the mountains to Alaska and Alberta. The plant illustrated was found on Healy Creek in Alberta, at an altitude of 6,000 feet.

Pl. 114. Tall Larkspur
Delphinium elongatum

Many species of *Delphinium* adorn the western states, as against the half-dozen found in the east. A distinction is commonly made by gardeners between the annual species, called Larkspur, and the perennial species, for which they reserve the name Delphinium; all belong to the genus *Delphinium*. There are 5 colored sepals in the flowers of this genus, of which the uppermost bears a long often curved spur. The 2 or 4 petals are small, often hairy, and form what the grower speaks of as the "bee" of the flower. The stamens, pistils and pods resemble those of *Aquilegia*.

Tall Larkspur has leaves cut into about 7 parts, these again sharply cut and toothed. The buds are lavender, the open flowers dark purplish-blue.

Delphinium elongatum grows in the mountains from Colorado westward to Alberta. The plant shown came from the Clearwater River in Alberta, at an altitude of 4,500 feet.

[27]

Pl. 115. Dwarf Larkspur
Delphinium depauperatum

The Dwarf Larkspur grows only a foot or so high (*depauperatum* means "impoverished"; plants stunted by lack of water or nutrients are often spoken of as "depauperate"). It is more or less hairy. The flowers are blue or purple with a partly white "bee."

Dwarf Larkspur occurs in meadows and open forests high in the mountains from Idaho and Nevada to Washington, Oregon and California. The painting was made from specimens collected in Alberta, at an altitude of 6,000 feet, 25 miles from Lake Louise.

Pl. 116. Western Red Baneberry
Actaea arguta

The name Baneberry refers to the supposed poisonous quality of the fruit. The species has a form with white berries, here illustrated. The stem grows to a height of 2 feet or more from an underground rootstock. The leaves are cut into 3 parts, the parts again thrice divided, and these parts yet again divided; a single leaf, with all its small leaflets, may be 20 inches long; part of one leaf is shown in the painting. The flowers are small, having from 3 to 5 white sepals, small petals, many stamens and a single pistil (which is unusual in this family).

Actaea arguta is found in woods from South Dakota and Nebraska to Alaska and southward to New Mexico and California. Similar species are known in the eastern states; various species are known as Cohosh. The painting was made from a plant collected near Banff, Alberta, in Vermilion Pass, at an altitude of 4,000 feet.

Pl. 117. Tall Buttercup
Ranunculus acris

The flowers of *Ranunculus* usually have 5 green sepals and 5 colored petals; the petals may be yellow or white, and in many species look as if they had been waxed and polished; this is due to a curious arrangement of the cells just under the surface. There is usually a small nectar-gland near the base. Each of the numerous pistils becomes an achene, a one-seeded fruit like a minute nut. The achenes of *Ranunculus acris* are somewhat flattened, with a thickened edge. The plant reaches a height of 3 feet.

The Tall Buttercup came from Europe, but is now almost as much at home in the eastern United States. It grows in fields and roadsides from Labrador to North Carolina and westward to Minnesota, Kansas and Oklahoma.

Pl. 118. Avalanche Buttercup
Ranunculus suksdorfii

The cluster of pistils surrounded by stamens is plainly evident in the painting. The achenes of this species have long narrow beaks.

The Avalanche Buttercup, which has been recently classified as variety *suksdorfii* of *Ranunculus escholtzii,* grows in mountain meadows near timberline from Alaska to Washington in the Cascade

Mountains and eastward to Montana in the Rockies. The painting was made from plants found near Field, British Columbia, at an altitude of 7,000 feet.

Pl. 119. Rue Anemone
Anemonella thalictroides

The Rue Anemone may be distinguished from similar small plants in related genera by the cluster of tubers at the base of the stem or group of stems, as well as by the shape of the leaflets of its divided leaves. Petals are lacking; the sepals are white or pinkish; the pistils become achenes. Double flowers having extra cycles of sepals are fairly common.

Rue Anemone grows in woods from Maine to Florida and westward to Minnesota and Oklahoma. The plant illustrated was collected near Washington, D. C.

Pl. 120. Columbia Windflower
Anemone deltoidea

The flowering stems of *Anemone deltoidea* arise from slender creeping underground stems, and reach a height of a foot. There is usually a single basal leaf divided into 3; and 3 leaves at a point where the one flower-stalk originates. The flowers of *Anemone* have sepals but no petals, many stamens, and a round or thimble-shaped head of pistils which become achenes. Windflower is a translation of the Greek word Anemone.

The Columbia Windflower is found in coniferous forests in the mountains of Washington, Oregon and northern California. The painting was made in Mt. Rainier National Park, Washington.

Pl. 121. Globose Anemone
Anemone globosa

The flowering stems of this species rise to a height of nearly 2 feet from a stout underground stem; they are softly hairy. The leaves are cut in threes, with the divisions 3-divided and again 3-divided. The sepals vary in color from greenish-yellow to pinkish or bluish. A young globose head of achenes is shown in the painting; when mature they are hairy.

Anemone globosa grows in open forests or on high open slopes from Alaska to northern California and eastward to Saskatchewan, South Dakota and Colorado. The illustration shows plants found at an altitude of 5,000 feet on Mt. Massive, near Banff, Alberta.

Pl. 122. Northern Anemone
Anemone parviflora

Northern Anemone has a one-flowered stem only a foot high or less, arising from a slender underground stem. The long-stalked basal leaves are 3-parted. The sepals vary from white to pink-tinged or purplish. In fruit, the cluster of achenes, usually densely hairy, is nearly half an inch long.

Anemone parviflora grows in moist places from Labrador to Alaska and southward to Quebec, Wisconsin, Colorado and eastern Oregon. The painting was made from plants which grew at an altitude of 7,000 feet 25 miles from Lake Louise, Alberta.

[28]

Pl. 123, 124. Pasqueflower
Pulsatilla ludoviciana

The Pasqueflowers are often included in the genus *Anemone;* they differ in that the hairy styles remain attached to the fruits (achenes) and even enlarge, forming long feathery appendages; the head of fruits is illustrated in Plate 124. Like many species of Anemone they have an involucre of 3 leaves at the base of the flower-stalk; these leaves, as well as the basal ones, are very finely divided. Some German botanists have supposed that the leaves of the involucre are really primitive sepals, separated from the other parts of the flower, and the colored petal-like parts of the flower, usually called sepals, are really petals.

This Pasqueflower ranges in prairies and on mountain slopes from Wisconsin to Alaska and southward to Illinois and Texas; something very like it is found in Europe and Asia. The plants shown grew near Banff, Alberta; the plant of Pl. 123 on Sulphur Mountain at an altitude of 8,000 feet; that of Pl. 124 on the Ghost River at 4,500 feet.

Pl. 125, 126. Western Pasqueflower
Pulsatilla occidentalis

The strictly western species of *Pulsatilla* differs in having the sepals white instead of purple (or white lightly marked with blue); and in the involucral leaves, which are slightly stalked. Plate 125 shows plainly the large group of pistils surrounded by the numerous stamens.

Pulsatilla occidentalis occurs on mountain-sides from Alaska to California, extending eastward in the high mountains to Montana and Utah. The painting of Plate 125 was made from plants that grew on Lake O'Hara near Lake Louise, Alberta, at an altitude of 4,000 feet; that of Plate 126 at the head of Johnson Creek, Alberta, at 8,500 feet.

Pl. 127. Hepatica *Hepatica americana*

The name is derived from the Greek word meaning "liver," in allusion to the shape of the leaves. This is also one of several different species which are known as Spring Beauty and Mayflower in some parts of the country. The leaves appear after the flowers and may be still green the following spring. The sepals vary from white to pink, lavender or purple. There are 3 green bracts simulating sepals a short distance below the flower. Another species has sharp-pointed leaf lobes.

Hepatica americana is found in woods from Nova Scotia and Quebec to Florida and westward to Manitoba, Minnesota, Missouri and Alabama. The plants sketched were found near Washington, D. C.

Pl. 128. Blue Jasmine *Clematis crispa*

About 150 species are known in the genus *Clematis,* besides many hybrids. They are climbing plants, the leaf-stalk often bending around a support, and sometimes forming tendrils in place of leaflets, as may be seen in Plate 128. The 4 or 5 sepals are often large and showy. There are no petals (or only some which re-

semble the numerous stamens). The head of fruit recalls that of *Pulsatilla*. The name Blue Jasmine for a species of *Clematis* may cause confusion, since Jasmine is the name of several very distinct species not related to each other or to this one (compare Bluebells, Plate 314; and Spring Beauty, Plates 104, 127). *Clematis crispa* has a somewhat bell-shaped flower, the sepals varying from nearly white to purple, their spreading parts having wavy thin margins. There are from 5 to 9 leaflets on each leaf stalk.

Clematis crispa grows in wet woods from Florida to Texas and northward to Virginia, Illinois and Missouri. The painting was made in Yemassee, South Carolina.

Pl. 129, 130. Virgin's Bower
Clematis columbiana

This species has 3 broad leaflets to a stalk. The flowers vary from blue to purple. A common eastern species, *Clematis virginiana,* is also called Virgin's Bower. It has rather small whitish sepals but a conspicuous head of fruit.

Clematis columbiana is found in forests from British Columbia to Oregon east of the Cascade Mountains and eastward to Alberta, Colorado and Utah. The paintings were made in British Columbia. Plate 129 was made from a plant collected near Field, on the slopes of Mt. Burgess, at an altitude of 6,500 feet; Plate 130 from plants found in Horse Thief Valley in the Selkirk Mountains, at 3,500 feet.

Pl. 131. Leather Flower *Clematis viorna*

This curious flower is distinguished by the thickness of its sepals; as the painting shows, they grow together so as to form an urn-shaped flower that is open only at the tip. Each leaf consists of from 3 to 7 leaflets. The head of fruit bears the usual decorative mass of plume-like styles.

Leather Flower grows in rich woods and thickets from Pennsylvania to Georgia and westward to Missouri and Texas. The plant illustrated grew near Washington, D. C.

Magnolia family.
Magnoliaceae

Of all the flowering plants of the present day, the Magnolias seem to come closest to the form which we suppose to have characterized the ancestors of the entire group. They are all woody, mostly tall trees. The flowers are borne singly at the ends of the branches. Flower parts are mostly numerous and to a certain extent are formed in a spiral (rather than in rings, cycles) upon a rather elongated central projection known as the receptacle. The pistils become 1- or 2-seeded pods. There are about 35 species of *Magnolia* in America and Asia, and many hybrids.

[29]

Most of them are valuable as ornamental trees.

All the paintings of this family were made from plants growing in Washington, D. C.

Pl. 132.   Sweet Bay   *Magnolia virginiana*

The leaves of this species are from 3 to 6 inches long and bluish-green on the under side. The bark is so attractive to beavers that the plant has been called Beaver Tree. The structure of the flower may be seen in the painting. The flowers are very fragrant; they measure two or three inches across.

Sweet Bay grows in swamps and wet ground from Massachusetts to Florida, westward on the coastal plain to Texas and Arkansas, and inland as far as Pennsylvania.

Pl. 133, 134.   Southern Magnolia
Magnolia grandiflora

This species is a tall tree, sometimes becoming 80 feet high. The branchlets and buds are noticeably rusty-looking with brown hairs. The leaves are as much as 8 inches long, and the fragrant white flowers 8 inches across. The sepals resemble the petals. Plate 134 shows the aggregate of fruits: the pods are attached to the elongated receptacle and open in that position, freeing the red seeds which hang for a time by long threads.

Magnolia grandiflora grows mostly in sandy soil on the coastal plain from North Carolina to Florida and Texas. It is the state flower of both Mississippi and Louisiana.

Pl. 135.   Cucumber Tree
Magnolia acuminata

The leaves of the Cucumber Tree are relatively thin and reach a length of 10 inches. The tree may grow 90 feet high. The curious flowers have erect green petals only 2 or 3 inches long. The head of fruit is 3 or 4 inches high.

The Cucumber Tree is found in rich woods from Ontario and New York to Georgia and westward to Missouri, Oklahoma and Alabama.

Pl. 136.   Yellow Cucumber Tree
Magnolia cordata

The Yellow Cucumber Tree is often classified as a variety of *Magnolia acuminata*. It has smaller flowers with petals of a yellowish color. *Cordata* means "heart-shaped," and refers to the outline of some of the leaves.

Magnolia cordata is known in South Carolina, Georgia and Alabama, where it grows in rich woods.

Pl. 137.   Tulip Tree, Yellow Poplar
Liriodendron tulipifera

Tulip Tree grows to heights of over 100 feet with a straight, often unbranched, trunk. Besides its value in ornamental plantings, it yields a fine-grained soft wood used in making furniture. The leaves fall and new leaves appear all summer, which makes it not altogether desirable in open plantings. The flower has much the same structure as that of a Magnolia; there

[30]

are 3 sepals and 6 petals in 2 cycles. The pistils form flat, scale-like fruits which do not open and are liberated from the receptacle. Another species of this genus is native in China. Several fossil species show us that the genus is of great antiquity and may have contained more species in the past.

Tulip Tree grows, mixed with other species, from northern New England to Florida and westward to Michigan, Missouri and Louisiana.

Custard-apple family.
Annonaceae

Pl. 138.   Papaw   *Asimina triloba*

The flowers of Papaw appear in spring just before the leaves. Like the Tulip Tree, the Papaw has 3 sepals and 6 petals in 2 sets; the latter are dark purplish-brown in color. There are numerous stamens but only a few pistils, which become large pulpy edible fruits. These must not be confused with the tropical fruits also known as Papaw but which belong to an entirely different family. The fruits of *Asimina*, each containing many seeds, have a delicious odor but the flavor is disappointing. In the Ozark hills they are known as Poor Man's Banana. In parts of the range no fruit is formed. The tree is small, rarely more than 30 feet high.

Asimina triloba is found along streams in alluvial soil from New York to Florida and westward to Michigan, Nebraska and Texas. The painting was made from a plant on Plummer's Island in the Potomac River near Washington, D. C.

Barberry family.
Berberidaceae

Pl. 139.   Creeping Mahonia   *Mahonia repens*

The stem creeps over the ground, rising only 6 or 8 inches above the surface. The flowers are small, yellow, with usually 3 sepals and 3 petals, 3 stamens and a single pistil. Another species of this genus, *Mahonia aquifolium,* is commonly called the Oregon Grape because of its blue berries; it is the state flower of Oregon. The genus is not related to the Grapes but to the Barberries.

Mahonia repens grows in open pine forests from British Columbia to northeastern California on the eastern slopes of the Cascade Mountains, and eastward to Alberta, Nebraska and New Mexico. The painting was made from a plant growing in Sinclair Canyon, British Columbia, at an altitude of 3,500 feet.

Pl. 140.   Twinleaf   *Jeffersonia diphylla*

The flowering stalk of Twinleaf rises about 6 or 8 inches from the ground. The curiously divided leaves grow from the base of this stem. The flower usually has 4 sepals which disappear early, 8 petals, 8 stamens and one pistil. The fruit is a pod or capsule which opens by a lid. The genus *Jeffersonia* was named for Thomas Jefferson.

Twinleaf grows in woods from New York and Ontario to Iowa and southward to Maryland and Alabama. The plants illustrated grew on Plummer's Island in the Potomac River near Washington, D. C.

Pl. 141. May-apple *Podophyllum peltatum*

Though very different in general aspect from other members of the Barberry Family, May-apple has the same floral structure: 2 sepals, from 6 to 8 petals, a single pistil. The stamens are somewhat more numerous — from 12 to 18. The large stigma is visible in the painting. The pistil becomes a small green edible berry. A creeping stem grows beneath the ground, sending up either a single umbrella-shaped leaf, or a stem bearing 2 leaves and a flower at the junction of the leaf-stalks.

May-apple is found in woods and open places over a wide range from Quebec to Florida and westward to Minnesota and Texas. The plant illustrated grew near Washington, D. C.

Poppy family. Papaveraceae

Pl. 142. Mexican Poppy
Eschscholtzia mexicana

In some seasons this plant colors the landscape with bright orange (or occasionally white or pink) for the period of blooming. The flowers open only in sunlight. There are 2 sepals which fall when the flower opens, 4 petals, many stamens, 1 pistil; the pistil becomes a slender pod which splits into 2 halves when ripe, much as do the pods of the Mustard Family. The end of the flower-stalk forms a cup-shaped receptacle about the base of the flower.

Mexican Poppy is found on plains and mesas from western Texas to California, northward into Utah, southward into Sonora. Another species, *Eschscholtzia californica,* is familiar in cultivation. The painting was made near Tucson, Arizona.

Pl. 143. Bush Poppy
Dendromecon rigida

This evergreen shrub may grow to 8 feet in height. The plan of the flower is the same as that of the preceding species; and it has the same kind of pod for fruit.

Bush Poppy grows on dry ridges in California and Baja California.

Pl. 144. Bloodroot *Sanguinaria canadensis*

The name is derived not from the root but from the thick horizontal underground stem; the red color is due to an alkaloid which was used by the Indians as a pigment. One leaf appears in spring, wrapped around the single flower-stalk. There are 2 sepals which fall when the flower opens, and often 8 petals of 2 sizes; but usually the number and arrangement of petals are not so regular. There are many stamens, and a single pistil which forms a spindle-shaped pod.

Bloodroot is a familiar spring flower along streams and in the woods from Quebec to Florida and westward to Manitoba, Kansas and Texas. The illustration was made from a plant growing near Washington, D. C.

Fumitory family.
Fumariaceae

Pl. 145. Pale Corydalis
Corydalis sempervirens

The Fumitory Family is related to the Poppies. Its flowers have 2 sepals and 4 petals, 6 stamens, and a narrow pod like that of a Mustard. The petals are in 2 pairs. In *Corydalis* the upper petal of the outer pair has a hollow spur which projects backward over the flower stalk. The 2 inner petals cohere at their tips and bear a projecting wing. The stamens are in 2 groups of 3 each, the stalks united in each group. Other species of *Corydalis* have yellow flowers.

Pale Corydalis has a wide range from Newfoundland to Georgia and westward to Alaska; it grows in open rocky places. The plant illustrated grew in the valley of the Kootenai River in British Columbia, at at altitude of 4,000 feet.

Pl. 146. Squirrel Corn
Dicentra canadensis

Dicentra differs from *Corydalis* in having both of its outer petals spurred; the spurs in this species are short and broad. The ends of these petals spread apart to disclose the crested joined tips of the inner pair. At the base of the stem is the short underground stem covered with yellow tubers, the "squirrel corn."

Dicentra canadensis grows in woods from Nova Scotia and Quebec to North Carolina and westward to Minnesota and Missouri. The plant in the sketch was collected near Washington, D. C. Another member of this genus is the familiar Bleeding Heart often seen in gardens.

Pl. 147. Dutchman's Breeches
Dicentra cucullaria

The leaves of this and the previous species are much the same, finely divided and pale bluish-green. *Dicentra cucullaria* has smaller tubers, and its 2 spurs are much longer; the crests of the inner petals are minute. The plant is said to be poisonous to livestock.

Dutchman's Breeches is found in woods from Nova Scotia and Quebec to Georgia and westward to North Dakota, Kansas and Arkansas. The plant illustrated grew near Washington, D. C.

Mustard family. Cruciferae

Pl. 148. Toothwort *Dentaria laciniata*

The Cruciferae are the Mustard Family. The flower of any member of the family (with a few exceptions) is easily recognized by its cross-like pattern (Crucifera means "cross-bearer") and numerical regularity. There are 4 sepals and 4 petals, commonly white or yellow; 6 stamens of which 4 are longer than the other 2; and a single pistil which becomes a two-chambered pod, splitting lengthwise into two halves when ripe. The family is important economically, for it includes all the Cabbages, Turnip, Mustard, Radish, Watercress, besides some troublesome weeds and such ornamental plants as Candy-Tuft and Stocks. *Dentaria* grows from an underground stem which is pinched here and there so as to make a string of small tubers. These are sometimes eaten and have a peppery taste more or less characteristic of the entire family.

Dentaria laciniata grows in woods and on banks from Quebec to Florida and westward to Minnesota, Nebraska, Kansas and Louisiana. The painting was made from a plant collected near Washington, D. C.

Pl. 149, 150. Bladder-pod *Physaria didymocarpa*

This is a typical crucifer of high and dry ground in the western states; the thick taproot remains alive from season to season; the close cluster of bluish leaves are not too open to the rigors of the climate. A magnifier discloses that the hairs of this plant are stellate, composed of radiating arms which make them star-like. *Physaria* means a bellows; *didymocarpa* means twin-fruit; both words refer to the inflated pod, shown in Plate 150, which has a lengthwise constriction dividing it into two lobes.

This Bladder-pod is found from Saskatchewan to Colorado and westward to Alberta and Utah. The specimen illustrated was collected at Lake Minnewonka near Banff, Alberta, at an altitude of 4,500 feet.

Pitcher-plant family. Sarraceniaceae

The Sarraceniaceae are the Pitcher-plants. The 3 genera in the family have about 10 known species (besides many hybrids), all American and mostly North American. They are characterized by leaves shaped like pitchers, tubes, or trumpets. In the largest genus, *Sarracenia,* the inner surface of these leaves exudes a juice which contains digestive enzymes. The outer surface produces nectar. The structure of the cells and the presence of down-pointing hairs around and beneath the lip on the inner surface ensure that small insects attracted by the nectar will fall into the pitcher

or tube and be unable to escape. Their bodies are digested in the liquid inside and the products are absorbed by the leaf, which is therefore carnivorous. The flower consists of 5 sepals and 5 petals, many stamens, and a curious 5-rayed umbrella-like structure in the middle which arises from the ovary and bears the stigmas on its margin. The fruit is a 5-chambered pod containing many seeds. All the species of this family described below grow in swamps, bogs, or other wet places.

The paintings were made (unless another source is given) from plants grown in the greenhouses of the U. S. Department of Agriculture in Washington, D. C.

Pl. 151. Pitcher-plant *Sarracenia purpurea*

This is the widest-ranging and commonest species of the genus, growing from Labrador to Florida and westward to Saskatchewan, Iowa and Mississippi (the northern and southern plants are placed in separate varieties). It is the national flower of Newfoundland. Its pitchers are curved and broadly winged, up to 10 inches long. The sepals and petals vary from greenish to purple.

Pl. 152. Sweet Pitcher-plant *Sarracenia rubra*

The right-hand flower in the painting has lost its petals and the "umbrella" in the center is visible. The flowers are very fragrant. The erect pitchers reach a height of 20 inches. The species grows from North Carolina to western Florida, mostly on the coastal plain.

Pl. 153. Hybrid Pitcher-plant *Sarracenia catesbaei*

This striking plant is a natural hybrid between *Sarracenia purpurea* and *Sarracenia flava,* and the specimen used for illustration was originally collected from a swamp near Quincy, Florida, where both the parental species were growing. There is evidence that the hybrid can perpetuate itself as if it were a good species. The plant was first described and named by the famous English botanist John Ray, in the seventeenth century.

Pl. 154. Purple-trumpet *Sarracenia drummondii*

The Purple-trumpet has erect leaves as tall as 30 inches. The flowers vary from greenish to deep purple. It grows from Georgia to Florida and Mississippi on the coastal plain.

Pl. 155. Yellow Pitcher-plant *Sarracenia flava*

Yellow Pitcher-plant is distinguished by the color of its petals. The leaves are erect and trumpet-shaped and may be over 30 inches tall; their hoods also may be bright yellow. The species is found abundantly from Virginia to Florida and Alabama.

Pl. 156. Hooded Pitcher-plant
Sarracenia minor
The lid, which in other species stands more or less erect, in this species is hood-like and curved over the opening of the long narrow pitcher. The leaves reach a length of 2 feet. *Sarracenia minor* grows from southern North Carolina to northern Florida on the coastal plain. The specimen used for illustration was found near Beaufort, South Carolina.

Pl. 157. Parrot Pitcher-plant
Sarracenia psittacina
The numerous small pitchers (6 inches long or less) of the Parrot Pitcher-plant are curved, partly reclining on the ground, with the opening hooded. They are marked with purple or red. The flowers vary from greenish to purple. The species is found in the pine barrens of Georgia and northern Florida and westward to Louisiana.

Pl. 158. Cobra Plant
Chrysamphora californica
The tall pitchers grow up to 30 inches high. Their ends curve so that the opening is directed downward. Nectar-glands are present on the exterior of the tube and on the 2-lobed appendage which extends out from the opening. Digestion of insects which fall into the tube is brought about by bacteria in the liquid inside; the products of this putrefaction are absorbed by the leaf. The flower is much like that of *Sarracenia* except for the much smaller size of its 5-rayed stigma and style.

Chrysamphora is the only pitcher-plant found in the western states. It grows in southern Oregon and northern California but not in the far northwest. The painting was made from a plant found in a bog in northern California.

Sundew family. Droseraceae

Pl. 159. Venus' Fly-trap
Dionaea muscipula
The leaves of *Dionaea* are the fly-traps. Each half of the blade bears 3 rather large hairs, clearly visible in the painting; the surface is glandular and forms nectar attractive to insects. When an insect touches one of the hairs, the 2 halves of the leaf are folded rapidly together (as if the midrib were a hinge) and the long teeth at the margin interlock, so that the visitor is now a prisoner. The leaf then exudes a fluid which brings about the digestion of the animal body; the products of this digestion are absorbed by the leaf. After about 10 days the halves move slowly apart again. The flowers have their parts in fives.

Another genus of insect-catching plants belongs in this family: *Drosera*, Sundew.

Venus' Fly-trap grows in bogs and pinelands on the coastal plain in North and South Carolina. The painting was made from a plant growing in a greenhouse of the U. S. Department of Agriculture in Washington, D. C.

Saxifrage family. Saxifragaceae

Pl. 160. Fringed Parnassia
Parnassia fimbriata
The petals are narrowed to a short stalk or claw, and are beautifully fringed on the sides, so that the green sepals underneath are visible in a delicate pattern in the center of the flower. A similar fringing or division of the petals is seen also in other members of this family. There are 5 petals, 5 sepals and 5 stamens; the ovary has but one cavity but bears 4 stigmas, not elevated on a style. The fruit is a capsule. Species of this genus are sometimes known as Grass of Parnassus, though of course they are not grasses.

Parnassia fimbriata grows in wet places high in the mountains from Colorado and Utah to Alaska and California. The painting was made from plants collected at Lake O'Hara near Hector, British Columbia, at an altitude of 6,000 feet.

SAXIFRAGE   SAXIFRAGA

There are about 250 species of Saxifrages, found mostly in the north temperate zone and farther north; some 65 species are known in North America. Their parts are generally in fives — 5 sepals, 5 petals, 10 stamens, with the stem tip (receptacle) often extending up around the ovary like a cup. The ovary has 2 chambers and is more or less divided into 2 lobes, with a style arising from each; the fruit is a small 2-beaked pod or capsule. The name means "rock-breaker," and was given to them probably because many of them grow in crevices.

Pl. 161. Red-stemmed Saxifrage
Saxifraga lyallii
The leaves are all basal. Not only is the stem red, but the reflexed sepals and the stamens as well; the petals are pink or white. The flowers are often double.

This Saxifrage grows on rocky ledges from Montana to Alaska and southward to Washington. The plant illustrated was found at Baker Lake near Lake Louise, Alberta, at an altitude of 6,500 feet.

Pl. 162. Purple Saxifrage
Saxifraga oppositifolia
As the painting shows, this species forms mats of creeping stems covered densely with small leaves. A single flower grows at the end of each branch.

It grows in rocky places and on cliffs from Greenland to Alaska and southward to northern New England, Wyoming and Oregon; also in Europe and Asia. The plants illustrated came from Fossil Mountain near Lake Louise, Alberta, at an altitude of 8,000 feet.

Pl. 163.   Tufted Saxifrage
Saxifraga caespitosa

The stems of this little plant are only 2 or 3 inches tall, and the flower-stalk no more than 4 inches. It is found high on rocky slopes or cliffs from Greenland to Alaska and southward to Newfoundland, Quebec, Arizona and Oregon; also far to the north in Europe and Asia. The painting was made from plants growing near Lake Louise, Alberta, at an altitude of 7,000 feet.

Pl. 164.   Spotted Saxifrage
Saxifraga austromontana

This is another species which forms a matted mass of horizontal stems and narrow leaves. The red flower-stalks grow up to 6 inches high, each bearing a cluster of small flowers. The white petals are veined and spotted with dark red.

Spotted Saxifrage grows among rocks in the mountains from Alberta to Alaska and southward to New Mexico and Oregon. The plants shown were collected near Lake Louise, Alberta, at an altitude of 6,500 feet.

Pl. 165, 166.   Prickly Currant   *Ribes lacustre*

The Currants and Gooseberries form the genus *Ribes;* some botanists place them in separate genera; sometimes also they are separated from the Saxifrages and placed in a family of their own. In general the flower is like that of a Saxifrage: 5 sepals, 5 petals, 5 stamens; the ovary has but one chamber but bears a 2-cleft style. The distinctive features are that the ovary is wholly inferior, with the receptacle adhering around it and extending above it in the form of a cup or tube; and that the fruit is a berry. The stem bears bristles and spines; the latter occur just under the lateral branches, taking the place of the leaves which we should expect to find there. In this respect this Currant resembles the Gooseberries.

Prickly Currant grows in mountain meadows from Newfoundland to Alaska, extending southward to Massachusetts, Pennsylvania, Michigan, Colorado, Utah and California. The plants illustrated were collected in British Columbia; the flowering plant on the slopes of Mt. Wapta near Field, at an altitude of 7,000 feet; the fruiting specimen near Glacier Lake, at 6,000 feet.

Witch Hazel family. Hamamelidaceae

Pl. 167.   Witch Hazel
Hamamelis virginiana

This plant has nothing to do with witches; the common name is derived from an Old English word meaning "pliable" and related to "weak." The use of

the branches as divining rods for finding water is well known. The extract of the same name is obtained from the bark. The flowers resemble those of the preceding family in many ways: 4 sepals, 4 petals, 8 stamens, and an ovary (partly inferior) which becomes a 2-chambered, 2-beaked pod. The narrow petals are characteristic. This species flowers in the autumn after the leaves have been shed; other species (one found in the Midwest) flower in winter or early spring.

Witch Hazel grows along streams and in moist woods from Nova Scotia and Quebec to Florida and westward to Minnesota and Texas. The plant illustrated, which bears flowers and old pods, grew near Washington, D. C.

Rose family. Rosaceae

The great Rose Family includes many well-known cultivated plants: Roses, Strawberries, Blackberries, Raspberries, Plums, Peaches, Cherries, Almonds. Sepals and petals are usually in fives, and grow, with numerous stamens, from the outer part of a cup or disc formed from the end of the flower-stalk and often called the receptacle. There are several or many pistils (one in *Prunus*). The leaves are usually attached singly, and each has a pair of small leaf-like appendages at the point where is joins the stem; these are the stipules.

Pl. 168.   Hardhack   *Spiraea tomentosa*

The small flowers grow in a long spike-like cluster. The leaves are white and woolly on the under side, where also the veins are prominent. The fruits of *Spiraea* are small pods which open along one side. Other species of the genus are Bridal Wreath and Meadow-sweet.

Hardhack grows in meadows, old pastures, and wet places from Nova Scotia and New Brunswick to North Carolina and westward to Minnesota and Arkansas.

Pl. 169.   Bowman's Root   *Gillenia trifoliata*

This species also has fruits composed of small pods. The narrow petals are characteristic. Another and similar species has large stipules, whereas those of *Gillenia trifoliata* are small and soon wither away.

Bowman's Root grows in upland woods from Ontario to Georgia and westward to Kentucky and Alabama. The painting was made from a plant near Washington, D. C.

Pl. 170.   Shrubby Cinquefoil
Potentilla fruticosa

Cinquefoil means "five-leaves"; the species of *Potentilla* are sometimes called Five-finger. *Potentilla* refers to a supposed potency in medicine, apparently without basis. Of the many American species of this genus, only two are shrubby, and one of these has white flowers. The Shrubby Cinquefoil grows to a height of about 3 feet.

Potentilla fruticosa grows in bogs and on wet slopes from Labrador to Alaska and southward to New Jersey, Ohio, Illinois, Minnesota, South Dakota, Arizona and New Mexico; also in Europe and Asia. The plant shown was collected near Field, British Columbia, in Burgess Pass at an altitude of 5,000 feet.

Pl. 171. Glaucous Cinquefoil
Potentilla glaucophylla

Some species of *Potentilla* may be mistaken for Buttercups, but the stipules and the expanded receptacle from which the perianth grows distinguish them. "Glaucous" refers to the bluish or grayish cast of the leaves of this species.

Glaucous Cinquefoil is found in mountain valleys from Saskatchewan to British Columbia and south through the Rockies to New Mexico and Utah. Several similar species grow in the eastern states. The painting was made from a plant collected at Lake O'Hara near Hector, British Columbia, at an altitude of 6,000 feet.

Pl. 172. One-flowered Cinquefoil
Potentilla uniflora

This is a typical mountain species, the stems, only 2 inches tall, forming dense tufts. The leaves are silky on the upper side, white and woolly beneath. The flower-stalks occasionally bear 2 flowers.

Potentilla uniflora grows from Alaska to the Hudson Bay region and southward to Oregon and Colorado; also in eastern Asia. The tuft of plants illustrated was found on a rocky slope in the Sawback Range near Banff, Alberta, at an altitude of 7,000 feet.

Pl. 173, 174. White Dryad *Dryas octopetala*

In spite of its botanical name, which means "8-petaled dryad," this species has from 8 to 10 petals. The Dryads are distinguished from several related genera by their simple leaves (i.e., they are not divided into several leaflets on one stalk, as are those of *Potentilla*). The White Dryad has leaves which are white and woolly, with prominent veins on the under side. The flower-stalk bears its single flower as much as 8 inches above the ground. Plate 174 shows the head of fruits with their hairy styles, like those of *Clematis* and *Pulsatilla*.

The White Dryad grows on high rocky ridges from Greenland to Alaska and southward to Colorado; also in Europe and Asia. The specimens illustrated came from Alberta; the flowering plant from the Skoki Valley near Lake Louise, at an altitude of 7,500 feet; the fruiting plant from the Siffleur River, at 6,500 feet.

Pl. 175, 176. Yellow Dryad
Dryas drummondii

This species is very similar to the preceding except for the color of its petals. It grows on rocky ledges and slopes from Quebec to British Columbia and southward to Montana and Oregon. The flowering plant was found in the Ice River Valley of British Columbia, 3,500 feet above sea level; the fruiting specimen came from the Siffleur River in Alberta, at the same altitude. The spiral arrangement of the unripe fruits and the sepals is well shown.

Pl. 177. Prairie Smoke *Sieversia triflora*

Notice that *Sieversia* has not only petals and sepals but a third ring of parts; these are called bractlets. The very long styles on the fruits are hairy except at the tip. The petals vary in color from yellowish to purple. The whole plant is softly hairy and fringed with long cilia ("eyelashes").

It grows in prairies and rocky places from New York to British Columbia and southward into Illinois, Iowa, Nebraska, New Mexico and California. The eastern and western plants are placed in separate varieties of the species.

Pl. 178. Pale-leaved Strawberry
Fragaria glauca

The flower of a Strawberry has a ring of bractlets like those of *Sieversia*. The so-called fruit, the edible berry, is the enlarged and succulent receptacle in the center of the flower, and the so-called seeds which are found upon it are the fruits formed from the numerous pistils.

Fragaria glauca is found in the mountains from British Columbia to New Mexico and eastward to South Dakota. It closely resembles *Fragaria virginiana,* which is the common wild strawberry growing in meadows and on hillsides in the eastern states. The cultivated strawberry is of hybrid origin. The specimen illustrated was collected on Baker Creek near Lake Louise, Alberta, at an altitude of 5,000 feet.

BLACKBERRY AND RASPBERRY *RUBUS*

The large genus *Rubus* is one of the most difficult to understand. Botanists cannot even agree on what to call a species; one recent manual lists 205 species from northeastern North America, another only 24 — from almost the same range. The so-called berry is really a cluster of small succulent stone-fruits, each having the structure of a cherry, and each developed from one of the many pistils in the center of the flower. In the raspberries the entire cluster of fruits slips off from the receptacle, the knob which bears it; in the blackberries the small fruits fall singly from the receptacle.

Pl. 179. Thimbleberry *Rubus parviflorus*

This species is a shrub, reaching a height of 6 feet. The leaves differ from those of most species of *Rubus* in being merely lobed, not divided. The fruit is red and edible.

Thimbleberry grows in open woods and thickets from Ontario to Alaska and southward to Colorado and California. The painting was made near Glacier, British Columbia, at an altitude of 3,500 feet.

[35]

Pl. 180. Flowering Raspberry
Rubus odoratus

This is the southern and eastern counterpart of *Rubus parviflorus,* differing from it in its rose-purple petals and its almost inedible fruit; it is also beset with sticky hairs. Both these species lack thorns.

Rubus odoratus occurs in thickets from Nova Scotia and Maine to North Carolina and westward to Michigan and Tennessee.

Pl. 181. Highbush Blackberry
Rubus argutus

The canes of many species of *Rubus* live for 2 years, flowering and fruiting the second year; the leaves of the first season may differ from those of the second. *Rubus argutus* has leaves divided into 5 leaflets the first season; on the flowering canes the leaves are divided into 3 only. The plant has few thorns.

This species grows in thickets from Georgia to Arkansas and northward into Massachusetts, Kentucky and Illinois. The plant shown was found near Washington, D. C.

Pl. 182. Red Dewberry   Rubus pedatus

The Dewberries are creeping species often found in old fields and on roadside banks. *Rubus pedatus* is a western representative of this group. It grows from Alaska to California and eastward to Alberta and Idaho. The plant illustrated was found in the valley of the Vermilion River, Alberta, at an altitude of 6,000 feet.

Pl. 183. Chickasaw Plum
Prunus angustifolia

The plums, cherries, peaches and almonds are usually all placed in the same genus *Prunus*. This differs from most other genera of *Rosaceae* in having but one pistil, which forms a stone-fruit (the seed is within the stone, which is formed from the inner layers of the ovary). The deep cup formed by the end of the flower-stalk, the receptacle, is plainly seen in the painting. This species is usually a shrub, occasionally a small tree reaching a height of about 12 feet. The fruit is red or yellowish and lacks the waxy bloom usually found on the plums; it is only about half an inch in diameter. The branchlets are sharp-pointed, becoming spines; this shows that it is a plum rather than a cherry.

Chickasaw Plum is found in sandy soil in fence rows and open woods from Newfoundland to Florida and westward to Indiana, Kansas and Texas. The painting was made at Washington, D. C.

Pl. 184, 185. Wild Rose   Rosa bourgeauiana

The flower of a Rose has its parts borne in or on a deep cup-shaped receptacle (like that of *Prunus*). There are many pistils, each becoming a hard seed-like fruit; and the entire receptacle becomes enlarged and succulent, a favorite food for birds and sometimes used by man.

There are many wild species of *Rosa,* often diffi-

cult to identify. *Rosa bourgeauiana* grows in woods from Ontario westward to Mackenzie and Colorado. The plants illustrated were found in Alberta; the flowering one at Lake Minnewonka near Banff, at an altitude of 4,500 feet; the fruiting plant in Sinclair Canyon, at 3,000 feet.

Apple family. Malaceae

The Apple Family is often united with the Rose Family; it is distinguished in having an inferior ovary. The ovary as usual becomes the fruit, but the enveloping parts of the stem-tip furnish most of the succulent tissue, the apple.

Pl. 186, 187. Red Chokeberry
Aronia arbutifolia

The Chokeberries are closely related to the Apples; they differ in the larger and branched flower-clusters, and in the finely toothed leaves which resemble those of a cherry. This species has about 20 red-tipped stamens (shown in Plate 186) and woolly branchlets and leaves. The fruit, like an apple formed from an inferior ovary, is only about ¼ inch in diameter. Chokeberry is a shrub usually about 6 feet tall.

Aronia arbutifolia grows in swamps and wet woods from Nova Scotia to Florida and westward to Texas, mostly on the coastal plain. Both the illustrations were made near Washington, D. C.

Pl. 188. Wild Sweet Crab   Malus coronaria

This is the common Wild Crab of the northeastern states; other species are found in the Southeast and Midwest. It is a tree 20 feet or more high. The 5 petals, 5 sepals and numerous stamens all seem to grow from the summit of the inferior ovary; the latter becomes the crabapple, which is still crowned by the withered sepals and stamens. The 5 styles are separate nearly to the base. The leaves are rather coarsely toothed, often slightly lobed.

Malus coronaria is found in open woods and thickets from New York to Georgia and westward to Michigan, Kansas and Alabama. The painting was made near Washington, D. C.

Pl. 189. Western Mountain Ash
Sorbus scopulina

Sorbus differs from *Malus* in having the leaves divided into many small leaflets arranged along either side of the long midrib (pinnately divided; i.e., like a feather). The cluster of small flowers is ample and branched; each flower resembles that of *Malus,* except in having only 2 or 3 styles, and the fruit also resembles a small apple, only about 1/3 inch across. This species is a shrub.

Sorbus scopulina is a shrub about 10 feet tall; it grows on hillsides and in ravines from Alberta and British Columbia to New Mexico and Arizona. The painting was made from a plant growing on Vermilion Summit near Castle Station, Alberta, at an altitude of 5,000 feet.

Pl. 190. Service-berry, Shad-bush
Amelanchier alnifolia

Amelanchier is distinguished from the other members of the family by having its ovary and fruit divided into 10 chambers, each containing only one seed. The styles, however, are usually 5. The petals are much narrower than in the other genera. The fruit is at first red, turning purplish as it ripens. The flowers and fruit are arranged singly along a short branch rather than in a cluster.

This species of Service-berry (the name is often pronounced "Sarvice-berry") is a shrub which reaches a height of 20 feet. It ranges from Ontario to Saskatchewan and southward to Michigan, Iowa, Nebraska, Colorado and Oregon, along streams and in the borders of woods. There is a form with white fruit. The plant shown was found on the Horse Thief River in British Columbia, at an altitude of 3,000 feet.

Bean family. Leguminosae

The Bean Family is related to the Rose Family. It contains the Pea, Bean, Clover, Alfalfa, Sweet Pea, Lupine, Wisteria, Peanut, and many other species familiar in cultivation, besides numerous weeds. Most of the genera have irregular flowers (i.e., not radially symmetric) described as papilionaceous (butterfly-like): there are a standard, two wings and a keel; within the keel the 5 to 10 stamens surround the single pistil. The pistil becomes the pod, which usually splits into two halves, lengthwise, when ripe. Many genera, however, have flowers differing widely from this scheme, on which basis the family has been divided into three by some botanists.

Pl. 191. Partridge-Pea *Cassia fasciculata*

Cassia has a flower only slightly irregular, the 5 petals being a little unequal. There are 5 to 10 unequal stamens; some may be imperfect or of different colors from the others. Leaves and pods of some species are used medicinally under the name of Senna.

Partridge-pea is common in old fields and roadsides from Massachusetts and Ontario to Florida and westward to Minnesota, South Dakota and Texas.

Pl. 192. Redbud *Cercis canadensis*

The flowers of Redbud are distinguished from others of the family by having the upper petal enclosed by the others in the bud, and by having 10 separate stamens. The leaves, which appear later, are undivided and heart-shaped. The tree may grow to a height of 40 feet.

Redbud grows in moist woods from Connecticut to Florida and westward to Nebraska and Texas; also in Mexico. The painting is of a plant growing near Washington, D. C.

Pl. 193. Wild Lupine *Lupinus perennis*

This is the eastern species of a genus which is more common westward, where many species have been described. The Texas Bluebonnet, the state flower, is a lupine. The leaves are divided palmately, i.e., the leaflets radiate in a way suggestive of the fingers of a hand. The 10 stamens of the flower are all joined in a tube around the pistil.

Lupine grows usually in sandy soil from Maine to Florida and westward to Minnesota and Louisiana. The painting was made near Washington, D. C.

Pl. 194. Prairie Clover
Petalostemum purpureum

The flowers grow in a close head like that of clover, blooming from the base up. Each flower has a standard and 4 smaller petals all much alike which adhere to the tube formed by the 5 stamens. The pod contains only 1 or 2 seeds. *Purpureum* means "purple"; the crimson shown in the painting was formerly known as purple, and the latter word must be understood in this sense in old names of plants.

This species of *Petalostemum* grows in dry grassy places from Indiana to Alberta and southward to Kentucky, Arkansas, Texas and New Mexico. The plant illustrated was found on a prairie east of Glacier National Park, Montana.

Pl. 195. Golden Pea
Thermopsis rhombifolia

The plant may grow to the height of a foot. The flower has 10 stamens, not joined. It grows in sandy places from Nebraska to Colorado and Alberta. There is also a species found in the eastern states. The plant shown was collected near Medicine Hat, Alberta, at an altitude of 3,500 feet.

Pl. 196. Goat's Rue *Tephrosia virginiana*

The wings and the keel of *Tephrosia* are joined. There are 10 stamens more or less joined to form a tube (the uppermost may be separate). The leaves are usually silky on the upper side; the lower side, with the rest of the plant, may be quite densely hairy; but this feature is extremely variable. The species is noted also for its very tough, long roots.

Goat's Rue occurs in old fields and open woods, usually in sandy soil, from Massachusetts to Florida and westward to Minnesota and Texas. The specimen illustrated came from Washington, D. C.

Pl. 197. Milk-vetch *Astragalus bourgovii*

The very large genus *Astragalus* (perhaps 1,500 species) is especially abundant in the western states; the species are difficult to identify. The leaves are pinnately divided in the manner shown in the illustrations. The flowers are of the usual papilionaceous type, with 9 of the 10 stamens united to form a tube open along the top; the tenth stamen lies in this opening. The characteristic flower-clusters also are shown in the paintings. The pods are often thick and hard and in many species divided into two compartments, or

[37]

almost so, and deeply grooved on one or both edges. Some of the species with thick pods are called Ground-plum. A number of western species are poisonous and known as Loco-weed.

Astragalus bourgovii has a rather flat oblong pod about ½ inch long, bearing black hairs. It grows in the mountains from South Dakota to British Columbia. The plant illustrated was collected in Burgess Pass near Field, British Columbia, at an altitude of 7,500 feet.

Pl. 198. Alpine Milk-vetch
Astragalus alpinus
This species has a narrow tapering pod which, if cut across, has an outline like a heart upside-down; the groove along the lower edge nearly divides the pod in two lengthwise. It is covered with black hairs and is rather leathery.

Astragalus alpinus grows on gravelly banks in arctic regions around the world, in North America from Labrador to Alaska and southward into Vermont, Wisconsin, Colorado, Idaho and Alberta. The painting was made from a plant collected on Johnson Creek in Alberta at an altitude of 6,000 feet.

Pl. 199. False Loco-weed
Oxytropis gracilis
Oxytropis is very similar to *Astragalus,* and some of the species have the same poisonous properties and are called Loco-weeds. The leaves are generally erect and the flowering stems rise from the base of the plant. The keel is pointed. In this species the sepals are silky. The pod is almost 2-chambered and nearly an inch long.

Oxytropis gracilis grows in open woodlands from South Dakota to Idaho and Alberta. The plant illustrated was found on the Ghost River near Banff, Alberta, at an altitude of 3,500 feet.

Pl. 200. Showy Oxytropis
Oxytropis splendens
This species has very numerous leaflets which are covered with white hairs; the flower-cluster is similarly hairy, as is the pod. The latter is egg-shaped, nearly divided into 2 compartments, about ½ inch long.

Showy Oxytropis grows on prairies and hillsides from Minnesota to British Columbia and southward in the mountains to New Mexico. The specimen in the painting came from the Bow Valley near Banff, at an altitude of 4,000 feet.

Pl. 201, 202. Point Vetch
Oxytropis podocarpa
Point Vetch is an arctic or alpine species, bearing its leaves and flowers close to the ground. The sepals are white and hairy. The pod, as shown in Plate 202, is inflated, and covered with fine black hairs.

Oxytropis podocarpa grows from Labrador to Yukon and southward into Colorado and Idaho. The plants illustrated were collected in Alberta: the one in

flower in Wonder Pass near Mt. Assiniboine, at an altitude of 8,000 feet; the fruiting specimen at Bow Lake near Lake Louise at 7,800 feet.

Pl. 203. Wisteria   Wisteria frutescens
Most species of *Wisteria* come from eastern Asia; several are known in cultivation; 2 are natives of our southeastern states. *Wisteria frutescens* is a shrubby climber, its stems twining. The sickle-shaped keel encloses stamens arranged as in *Astragalus,* 9 joined and 1 separate. The smooth pod contains a few large seeds.

This *Wisteria* grows in moist woods and on river banks from southern Virginia to Florida and Alabama. The plant shown was found near Savannah, Georgia.

Pl. 204. Sweet Vetch
Hedysarum mackenzii
The pod of *Hedysarum* is compressed and composed of a series of joints, which easily separate. Those of *Hedysarum mackenzii* are round. Its flowers are usually described as purple, but the color varies to light shades and, as shown in the painting, even to white; they are very fragrant. Notice also the long sharp sepals. The roots have been used for food.

Hedysarum mackenzii grows on dry slopes, often among shrubs, in Arctic America, extending southward to Alberta and eastern Oregon; also to Newfoundland. The painting was made from plants growing near Lake Louise, Alberta, at an altitude of 8,000 feet.

Pl. 205. Vetch   Vicia americana
In flowers of Vetch the standard envelops the wings; the wings adhere to the keel, which is short. There are 10 stamens, 9 united to form a tube open along the upper side, the tenth free in this opening. The flowers are in small clusters (or sometimes singly borne) from the points where the leaves arise. The terminal leaflets of the leaf are often replaced by tendrils, by which the plant adheres to any support that is at hand. This species is recognized by its narrow leaflets and the stipules, which are coarsely toothed.

Vicia americana grows in moist woods and on gravelly shores from Quebec to Alaska and south to Virginia, Ohio, Arkansas and Oklahoma. The plant illustrated was collected near Banff, Alberta, at an altitude of 4,000 feet.

Pl. 206. Vetchling   Lathyrus ochroleucus
Lathyrus is very similar to *Vicia,* the distinction being in certain details of the stamens and pistil. The best-known species is *Lathyrus odoratus,* the Sweet Pea, a native of Europe. *Lathyrus ochroleucus* grows from a slender underground stem. The sepals form a very irregular cup, the upper side being much shorter than the lower. The large stipules and the tendrils are well illustrated in the painting.

Lathyrus ochroleucus grows in woods and on rocky banks from Quebec to British Columbia and southward to Pennsylvania, Ohio, South Dakota, Wyoming, Idaho and Oregon. The plant illustrated was found at Lake Minnewonka near Banff, Alberta, at an altitude of 4,000 feet.

Geranium family.
Geraniaceae

Pl. 207. Wild Geranium, Cranesbill
Geranium maculatum
The Geranium flower has a simple numerical pattern: 5 sepals, 5 petals, 10 stamens in 2 sets, and a pistil with a 5-chambered ovary and 5-cleft style. The styles form a beak to the fruit (*Geranium* is derived from the Greek word for heron or crane); at maturity it splits at the base into its 5 parts, and each part curls up and lifts one-fifth of the ovary, shedding the seed within.

This Wild Geranium is the commonest large eastern species. It is found in open woodlands from Maine to Georgia and westward to Manitoba, Kansas and Tennessee. The cultivated Geranium is *Pelargonium,* in the same family.

Pl. 208. Western Cranesbill
Geranium viscosissimum
This western species is known by the sticky hairiness of its flowers and flower-stalks. The leaves are hoary with dense whitish hairs. It grows from an underground stem.

Western Cranesbill grows in prairies and open woods from South Dakota to British Columbia and southward into Nevada and California. The plant illustrated was collected in the mountains northeast of Lake Louise at an altitude of 5,000 feet.

Milkwort family.
Polygalaceae

Pl. 209. Orange Milkwort
Polygala lutea
The *Polygala* flower is irregular: there are 5 sepals, the 2 lateral being much larger and colored like the petals; 3 petals, the lowest keel-like, all joined with each other and with the 6 or 8 stamens, which are also more or less united; the ovary has 2 chambers. The name refers, not to any milky juice, but to the reputed virtue of some species in increasing the flow of milk.

Orange Milkwort is found in pinelands and boggy places on the coastal plain from New York to Florida and Louisiana. The painting was made at Beaufort, South Carolina.

Pl. 210. Fringed Milkwort
Polygala paucifolia
This species differs from the preceding in having its flowers borne singly; they vary from red-purple to white. The keel petal is cut at the tip into narrow segments, forming a delicate fringe.

Fringed Milkwort grows in the mountains from Quebec to Georgia and westward to Manitoba, Minnesota, Illinois and Tennessee. The specimen illustrated was collected near Pocono Manor, Pennsylvania.

Crowberry family.
Empetraceae

Pl. 211. Crowberry *Empetrum nigrum*
The Crowberry suggests a Heath; but the flowers lack petals; there are 3 sepals and 3 stamens; the stigma has 6 to 9 rays.

Crowberry is found in boggy places in arctic regions around the world, extending southward in America to Newfoundland, New England, northern Michigan, Minnesota, Alberta and northern California. The plant sketched grew in Vermilion Pass near Castle Station, Alberta, at an altitude of 5,000 feet.

Holly family. Aquifoliaceae

Pl. 212. American Holly *Ilex opaca*
There are actually several species of American Holly. *Ilex opaca* most resembles the European, with its spiny evergreen leaves, and like that species is gathered for Christmas decoration. The tree may grow 50 feet tall. The flowers are small, greenish, with the parts in fours, some containing no pistils.

Ilex opaca grows in moist woodlands from Massachusetts to Florida and westward to Missouri and Texas. The painting was made at Washington, D. C.

Pl. 213. Yaupon, Cassena *Ilex vomitoria*
This is a shrub or small tree with thick evergreen leaves which are indented on the edges but not toothed. The flower parts are in fours. An infusion of the leaves is drunk like tea; if the brew is strong, it has emetic properties, whence the botanical name. The well-known South American drink maté is made from a species of *Ilex.*

Yaupon grows in sandy woodlands from southeastern Virginia to Florida and westward to Arkansas and Texas. The plant illustrated was found near Beaufort, South Carolina.

Pl. 214. Winterberry *Ilex verticillata*
Winterberry is a shrub about 10 feet high. The leaves are not spiny but finely toothed; they fall in the

[39]

autumn. The flowers and fruit grow in dense clusters (verticils), with their sepals, petals and stamens numbering 4 to 8. The plant is highly variable.

It grows in swamps and wet woods from Newfoundland to Georgia and westward to Minnesota, Missouri and Tennessee. The branch shown came from a plant growing near Washington, D. C.

Maple family. Aceraceae

Pl. 215. Red Maple *Acer rubrum*
The flowers of Red Maple are among the earliest flowers of spring, appearing long before the leaves. Staminate flowers are shown in the painting; other flowers have pistils only, and still others have both stamens and pistils. The petals are similar to the sepals in size and color. The 2-lobed ovary grows a pair of wings and becomes the maple "key," which in this species is also bright red. The leaves are palmately lobed, with sharp notches between the lobes, their under side whitish and often downy.

Red Maple has a wide range, from Newfoundland and Quebec to Florida and westward to Manitoba, Missouri and Texas; it is best developed in low woods and swamps. The specimen illustrated was collected at Spring Lake, New Jersey.

Pl. 216. Carolina Maple *Acer carolinianum*
Carolina Maple is perhaps only a variety of Red Maple. It is a smaller tree, with leaves that are usually only 3-lobed, sometimes not lobed at all. The painting shows the young "keys"; the leaf buds are just beginning to open.

The tree is found on the coastal plain from New Jersey to Florida and westward to Texas and Missouri. The painting was made at Beaufort, South Carolina.

Horse Chestnut family. Hippocastanaceae

Pl. 217. Red Buckeye *Aesculus pavia*
The Buckeyes have large irregular flowers: 5 sepals, 4 or 5 petals which are unequal in size, usually 7 stamens and a 3-chambered pistil which becomes a round leathery fruit. The fruit is prickly in some species, but not in this one. The seed is hard and shining, somewhat resembling a Chestnut; the Horse Chestnut comes from the European tree of the same name, from which the family name is taken. All the species have paired leaves divided palmately into several leaflets. Most of them have yellowish petals.

Red Buckeye grows in woods and thickets from Virginia to Florida and Louisiana. The painting was made at Beaufort, South Carolina.

[40]

Balsam family. Balsaminaceae

Pl. 218. Jewelweed, Touch-me-not
Impatiens capensis
The flowers of Jewelweed hang on their slender stalks. There are 3 sepals, the lower one petal-like and expanded into a sac which is prolonged backward into a bent hollow spur; and 3 petals. The 5-chambered ovary becomes a pod which splits open at a touch into 5 valves which curl up and scatter the seeds.

Jewelweed is an annual plant; it forms dense lush stands in ravines and along streams from Newfoundland to South Carolina and westward to Saskatchewan, Missouri and Oklahoma. It has been introduced into Europe. The Balsam grown in gardens is also in this genus.

Mallow family. Malvaceae

Pl. 219. Scarlet Globe-mallow
Malvastrum grossulariaefolium
The Mallows have numerous stamens united into a tube, through the top of which the branched style projects. In this species the mass of stamen heads is purplish-black. The ovary is composed of several segments, and when they are ripe, these separate into small one-seeded fruits; the seed occupies one end of the cavity, the other being empty. The hairs of Globe-mallow, as of many species in this family, are called "stellate"; as under a magnifier they are seen to be branched and have a star-like appearance.

Scarlet Globe-mallow grows in dry places from Idaho to Washington and southward to New Mexico, Arizona and California. The plant illustrated was found near Tucson, Arizona.

Pl. 220. Globe-mallow
Sphaeralcea davidsonii
Sphaeralcea differs from *Malvastrum* in that its seeds fill the cavities of the fruits. The petals of this species change to yellow as they age. The leaves are woolly with white hairs. It grows only in dry streambeds in southern California; the specimen painted was collected near Rancho Santa Ana.

Pl. 221. Rose Mallow
Hibiscus moscheutos
Rose Mallow is a shrub reaching a height of 6 feet. The genus *Hibiscus* is a large one, recognizable by the narrow bracts which surround the sepals and by the stamens which bear their heads at various levels along the tube instead of all at the tip. The ovary is composed of 5 segments and the style has 5 branches. Other species of *Hibiscus* are the Rose of Sharon, a

native of Asia, and Okra; other members of the family are Hollyhock and Cotton.

Hibiscus moscheutos grows in marshes, mostly near the coast, from Connecticut to Florida, Texas and Missouri.

St. John's Wort family. Hypericaceae

Pl. 222. Tall St. John's Wort
Hypericum pyramidatum

The St. John's Worts often have numerous stamens joined at their bases into a number of bunches; there are 5 such bunches in this species. The ovary has 5 chambers and 5 styles. The leaves contain glands which make translucent spots. In other species the petals are spotted with black glands. Some of these species are common roadside weeds.

The Tall St. John's Wort, which may grow to 6 feet in height, is found in moist meadows and thickets from Quebec to Maryland and westward to Manitoba and Kansas.

Sterculia family. Sterculiaceae

Pl. 223. Mexican Fremontia
Fremontia mexicana

This shrub is evergreen, as tall as 20 feet. The flowers have no petals, but 5 large sepals colored like petals; there are also small bracts outside the sepals. The 5 stamens are partly united. The 5-chambered ovary forms a pod which splits open in 5 lines. The leaves are densely covered on the under side with a felt of whitish hairs; these hairs are branched (stellate).

Fremontia mexicana grows in the open chaparral of southern California and southward into Mexico. The painting was made in Los Angeles. The species is closely allied to *Fremontia californica*.

Tea family. Theaceae

Pl. 224. Franklinia *Franklinia alatamaha*

Franklinia has had a curious history. It was discovered by John and William Bartram on the coastal plain in Georgia in 1765, and has never been seen growing wild since 1790; it has been widely cultivated. It is a tall shrub or tree, up to 30 feet high, which flowers in the autumn; the flowers are fragrant.

The plant illustrated was cultivated at Whitesbog, New Jersey.

Pl. 225. Stewartia *Stewartia malacodendron*

Stewartia is a shrub which grows up to 15 feet tall. The flower has many purple stamens. The ovary has several chambers but only one short style; the stigma is 5-toothed. The fruit is a woody pod.

Stewartia is rare in the wild state, though, like Franklinia, it is often cultivated. It grows on the coastal plain in rich woods from Virginia to Florida and westward to Arkansas and Louisiana. The plant illustrated was found on Lady's Island near Beaufort, South Carolina.

Violet family. Violaceae

VIOLET   VIOLA

The Violet flower has a lower petal which projects backward as a spur. There are 5 stamens which fit closely around the style, holding their pollen, as it were, in a basket; the 2 lower ones bear nectaries which extend into the spur. An insect penetrating into the spur must touch these projecting glands and disturb the stamens, which shed their pollen on the visitor; this pollen may be rubbed off on the stigma of the next flower visited. There are also flowers which never open but fertilize themselves; they grow usually near the base of the plant, and produce more fruit than the ordinary flowers. The ovary is not divided; it forms a small pod with 3 rows of seeds attached to the 3 valves into which it splits when ripe.

Pl. 226. Birdfoot Violet *Viola pedata*

The Birdfoot Violet belongs to the group known as "stemless" Violets; their stems are short and thick and grow underground. There are 2 forms of the species; in one the 2 upper petals are dark purple, as shown in the painting; in the other all the petals are light blue. The leaves also vary greatly in outline.

Viola pedata grows in open places, often on rocky slopes, from Maine to Florida and westward to Minnesota and Texas; in parts of the Midwest it is common. The painting was made near Washington, D.C.

Pl. 227. Southern Coast Violet
Viola septemloba

This is another of the "stemless" Violets. The earliest leaves are unlobed; the later leaves have the 7 lobes responsible for its name, the middle lobe being the largest. The flowers which do not open are on erect stalks.

Viola septemloba grows on the coastal plain in sandy soil and pinelands from Virginia to Mississippi. The illustration was made near Washington, D. C.

Pl. 228. Canada Violet *Viola canadensis*

Canada Violet has an erect leafy stem; the small stipules (paired appendages like minute leaves) may be seen at the base of the leaf-stalk. The petals are white inside with a yellowish center.

[41]

Viola canadensis grows in woods from Newfoundland to South Carolina and westward to Alberta and Arizona. The painting was made near Lake Louise, Alberta, at an altitude of 5,000 feet.

Pl. 229.   Smooth Yellow Violet
Viola eriocarpa

The leaves and stem of this species are smooth or almost so; the capsule may be woolly (this is the meaning of *eriocarpa*) or, in a variety, smooth.

Viola eriocarpa is found in woods and low meadows from Nova Scotia to Georgia and westward to Manitoba and Texas. The plant illustrated grew on Plummer's Island in the Potomac River near Washington, D. C.

Pl. 230.   Purple Violet   *Viola adunca*

The form of *Viola adunca* which grows in the eastern states has long stems which tend to lie on the ground. In the high mountains of the west this diminutive form is found which resembles one of the "stemless" blue Violets. The lowland form is downy, the mountain form smooth.

Viola adunca is found from Quebec and New England westward to Alaska and California. The plant illustrated was collected at Bow Lake near Lake Louise, Alberta, at an altitude of 6,000 feet.

Pl. 231.   Johnny Jump-up   *Viola rafinesquii*

The small flowers of this species vary greatly in color from almost white or yellowish to purple with a yellow "eye." The stipules are large and cut into narrow segments, giving the base of the leaf a feathery appearance.

Viola rafinesquii grows in fields and roadsides from New York to Georgia and westward to Colorado and Texas. In places it is so abundant that it colors the fields blue. The plant sketched grew in Rock Creek Park in Washington, D. C.

Passion Flower family. Passifloraceae

Pl. 232.   Maypops   *Passiflora incarnata*

The Passion Flowers were so named by early travelers who fancied they saw in the parts of the flower the implements used in the crucifixion; for instance, the fringe of colored filaments just inside the petals was thought to symbolize the crown of thorns; the 3 styles with their broad stigmas were nails; and so forth. The fruit is berry-like, as large as a hen's egg, fragrant and edible, structurally much like the pod of a violet. The common name comes from the sound made by the fruit when it is opened. This species climbs by means of coiling tendrils.

Maypops grows both in thickets and in the open from Virginia to Florida and westward to Oklahoma

and Texas. The illustration was made from a plant found near Savannah, Georgia.

Cactus family. Cactaceae

Many succulent or prickly plants are commonly known as Cactus; but the name is technically reserved for a family of American plants. The stems of these plants are much enlarged and contain considerable liquid; leaves are not formed, or only rudiments which fall early. The flowers have numerous sepals and petals in several rows and with the end of the stalk form a tube which not only invests the ovary but rises above it and bears the stamens on its inner surface. The ovary has but one cavity, and there is one style which supports a number of stigmas.

Pl. 233.   Prickly Pear   *Opuntia polyacantha*

Prickly Pears (there are several species) bear barbed spines. Leaves are formed on the leaf-like joints of the stem, but soon fall off. Some species have edible fruit, and are known as Tuna.

Opuntia polyacantha is found in dry prairies from Wisconsin and Minnesota westward to Alberta and southward to Missouri, New Mexico and Utah. The painting was made near Medicine Hat, Alberta, at an altitude of 3,500 feet.

Pl. 234.   Strawberry Cactus
Echinocereus lloydii

The name comes from the berry-like appearance of the small stem, which consists of a single segment. The fruit is edible, the spines being easily removed.

This species grows only in western Texas.

Pl. 235   Green-flowered Strawberry Cactus
Echinocereus viridiflorus

The stem of this species has about 13 ribs. The flowers are greenish-brown on the outside, greenish-yellow on the inside. The entire plant is only a few inches high. The small green fruits are edible.

Echinocereus viridiflorus grows in dry plains from Wyoming to Texas and New Mexico. The plant illustrated came from Texas.

Oleaster family. Elaeagnaceae

Pl. 236.   Buffalo Berry
Shepherdia canadensis

Buffalo Berry is a shrub about 6 feet tall. The leaves are smooth on the upper side, silvery and rather rusty with small scales on the lower side. The flowers are small, yellowish, either staminate or pistillate, the sepals 4. The so-called berry is actually formed by the sepals, which are joined and enclose the ovary. A related species has a better right to the name Buffalo Berry; it was much esteemed by the Indians for food.

Shepherdia canadensis grows in rocky or sandy places from Newfoundland to Alaska and southward to New York, Indiana, New Mexico and Arizona. The specimen illustrated was collected near Hector Station, British Columbia, at an altitude of 5,000 feet.

Pl. 237, 238. Silverberry
Elaeagnus commutata

Elaeagnus differs from *Shepherdia* chiefly in having stamens and pistils in the same flower, and in having the fleshy united sepals enclosing a hard nut-like fruit. Some Asiatic species are well known in cultivation under the names of Oleaster or Russian Olive.

Elaeagnus commutata grows on rocky hillsides from Quebec to Yukon and southward to Minnesota, Nebraska and Utah. The flowering specimen of Plate 237 was collected on the Ghost River in Alberta, at an altitude of 4,000 feet; the fruiting branch shown in Plate 238 came from the Kootenai River valley in British Columbia, at 3,000 feet.

Evening Primrose family. Onagraceae

Pl. 239. Evening Primrose
Oenothera biennis

The family is recognized by its generally 4-parted flowers with an inferior ovary. In *Oenothera* there are 4 reflexed sepals, 4 petals, 8 stamens; the style bears a 4-parted stigma; the pod splits into 4 parts. *Oenothera biennis* is a highly variable group of plants common in old pastures and roadsides; the dead stalks and dried pods are a familiar sight. It is found from Quebec to Florida and westward to Manitoba, Kansas and Texas.

Pl. 240. Evening Primrose
Pachylophus hirsutus

This Evening Primrose has almost no stem above the ground. The flowers are open in the evening and are then very fragrant. The pod has narrow wings extending from its 4 angles. The 4 stigmas characteristic of the family are very evident in the painting.

Pachylophus hirsutus is found on dry slopes at altitudes above 7,000 feet from Wyoming to New Mexico and Arizona and westward to Utah. The plant illustrated was collected near Roosevelt Dam in Arizona.

Pl. 241. Rock Rose
Pachylophus caespitosus

This species has a short stem above the ground. The pod is tubercled on the angles. Otherwise it is very similar to the preceding species. The form illustrated is a hairy variety; typical *Pachylophus caespitosus* is smooth. The genus *Pachylophus* is included by many botanists in *Oenothera*.

Pachylophus caespitosus grows on dry slopes from the Dakotas to Washington and southward to Arizona and California. The plant shown was found south of Tucson, Arizona.

Pl. 242. Fireweed   *Epilobium angustifolium*

This plant gets its name from its habit of springing up abundantly in burned areas, especially after forest fires. It is extremely variable. The petals may be white. The style is hairy near the base. The plant may reach a height of 6 feet. The word *angustifolium* refers to the narrow leaves.

Fireweed grows usually in moist soil throughout far northern America, Europe and Asia. In America it extends southward as far as New Jersey, Ohio, Illinois, Kansas and New Mexico. The plant illustrated came from the Clearwater River in Alberta, at an altitude of 6,000 feet.

Pl. 243. Broad-leaved Willow-herb
Epilobium latifolium

In this species the leaves are broader (*latifolium*) and those beneath the flowers, which in the preceding species are much reduced, are here more like the other leaves. The style has no hairs.

Epilobium latifolium is found on shores and ledges from Greenland to Alaska and southward to Newfoundland, Quebec, South Dakota, Colorado and Oregon; also in Europe and Asia. The painting shows a plant which grew near Glacier, British Columbia, at an altitude of 3,500 feet.

Pl. 244. Yellow Willow-herb
Epilobium luteum

The color of the flowers is unusual for this genus. They grow singly from the same points as the leaves rather than in a terminal spike. There are 2 series of stamens of different length, 4 of each. The protruded style is evident in the painting. The entire plant is smooth.

Yellow Willow-herb grows in wet places from Alaska to Oregon. The painting was made at Glacier, British Columbia, at an altitude of 3,500 feet.

Ginseng family. Araliaceae

Pl. 245. Devil's Club   *Oplopanax horridus*

Devil's Club is an ill-scented plant with sharp stiff spines that make it a serious problem to one who walks where it grows (*horridus* means "bristling" or "prickly"). The petals are greenish-white; sepals are lacking. There are 5 stamens and an inferior ovary with 2 styles.

Devil's Club is found by streams and in moist woods from Montana to Alaska and Oregon; also on Isle

Royale, Michigan. The plant illustrated grew near Field, British Columbia, at an altitude of 4,000 feet.

Dogwood family. Cornaceae

Pl. 246. Red-osier Dogwood
Cornus stolonifera

Cornus stolonifera is a tall shrub whose long red branches bend and root where they touch the ground, sending up new clusters of stems. The small white flowers have 4 sepals and 4 petals, 4 stamens and an inferior ovary which is 2-chambered. The fruit is a stone-fruit, with a stone containing 1 or 2 seeds. Flowers and fruit are formed continuously all summer. This species is distinguished from other shrubby Dogwoods by the large white pith seen when a branchlet is cut across.

Cornus stolonifera grows mostly along streams and in swamps from Newfoundland to New York, westward to Alaska and California, and southward into Mexico. The plant shown was collected at Radium Hot Springs, British Columbia, at an elevation of 3,000 feet.

Pl. 247, 248. Flowering Dogwood
Cornus florida

All Dogwoods have flowers; this species owes its common name to the clusters of flowers surrounded by 4 enlarged bud-scales (bracts) which resemble white petals. The individual small yellow flowers and red fruits are much like those of the preceding species in structure. The leaves also are characteristic of the genus: the veins leave the midrib near its base and curve forward parallel to the margin. Forms are known with pink and red "flowers," and one with yellow fruits. The wood is hard (which is the meaning of *Cornus*). A bitter principle obtained from the bark has been used as a tonic and in the treatment of malaria.

Flowering Dogwood grows in woods from Maine to Florida and westward to Kansas and Texas; a subspecies is found in Mexico; related species occur in the Pacific States and in Asia. The specimen used in making Plate 247 was found near Washington, D. C.; that shown in Plate 248, near Fairfax, Virginia.

Pl. 249, 250. Bunchberry, Dwarf Cornel
Cornus canadensis

Bunchberry sends up its shoots from a woody underground stem. The "flowers" are flower-clusters like those of Flowering Dogwood. The small true flowers are generally white; those illustrated are unusual in their red tint. There is also a form with pink bracts.

Bunchberry grows in moist acid soil in woods or bogs from Greenland and Labrador to Alaska and southward to New Jersey, Kentucky, Wisconsin, South Dakota, Idaho and California; also in northeastern Asia. The painting of the flowering speci-

men was made at Lake Louise, Alberta, at an altitude of 5,000 feet; the fruiting plant came from near Hector Station, British Columbia, at 4,500 feet.

Heath family. Ericaceae

The Heath Family has the sepals united into a tube or cup; the petals also are united, at least by their lower parts. The parts of a flower are usually in fours or fives. The fruit is a dry pod in most genera. The leaves are undivided, usually attached singly. Our species of this family are found mostly in boggy, acid soils, where their roots are probably associated with certain fungi, and are characteristic of high mountains and northern forests; many other species, however, are natives of the southern hemisphere and of the tropics.

Pl. 251. Labrador Tea
Ledum groenlandicum

Labrador Tea has an aromatic fragrance when it is bruised. The blunt evergreen leaves are densely woolly on the under side with whitish or rusty hairs. The small flowers are regular, with 5 to 7 stamens and a 5-chambered ovary. The plant grows about 3 feet high.

Labrador Tea grows in boggy soils from Greenland to Alaska and southward to New Jersey, Ohio, Michigan, Wisconsin, Alberta and Washington. The specimen illustrated was collected in the White Mountains of New Hampshire.

Pl. 252. Tar-flower *Befaria racemosa*

Tar-flower is an evergreen shrub reaching a height of 8 feet. There are 6 or 7 petals and sepals and twice as many stamens. The petals are separate almost to the base.

Tar-flower grows in pinelands on the coastal plain from Georgia to Florida. Its closest relatives are in Mexico and South America. The plant shown in the painting was gathered near Jacksonville, Florida.

RHODODENDRON AND AZALEA
RHODODENDRON

This large and well-known genus has often been divided into two: *Rhododendron*, with evergreen leaves; and *Azalea*, which sheds its leaves in winter. The sepals are very small. The petals are joined at the base, and often differ in size and shape, so that the flower is irregular. There are 5 or 10 long stamens; the pollen is discharged through pores in the ends instead of through a split. The 5-chambered ovary bears a long style. The species have hybridized freely both in nature and in cultivation, and are difficult to identify.

Pl. 253. Rose Bay *Rhododendron maximum*

Rose Bay may form shrubs or small trees up to 30

feet tall. The thick evergreen leaves are almost smooth. The species occurs in moist woods from southern Ontario to Georgia and westward to Ohio and Alabama; it is more abundant in the southern part of its range. The plant illustrated was obtained from the mountains of North Carolina.

Pl. 254.　White-flowered Rhododendron
Rhododendron albiflorum

The flowers, instead of forming a terminal group as in most of the species, are in lateral clusters. The leaves are rather rusty, with loose hairs; they are deciduous. The plant grows on mountain slopes near timberline from British Columbia to northern Oregon and eastward to the Rocky Mountains. The specimen illustrated was found near Glacier, British Columbia, at an altitude of 3,500 feet.

Pl. 255.　Smooth Azalea
Rhododendron arborescens

This species is a tall shrub or a tree up to 20 feet high, almost free from any hairiness. The petals are white or pink. The 5 stamens and the long style are clearly shown in the painting. Smooth Azalea grows in upland woods from Pennsylvania to Georgia and westward to Kentucky and Alabama. The plant illustrated was found near Linville, South Carolina, at the foot of Grandfather Mountain.

Pl. 256.　Pinkster-flower
Rhododendron nudiflorum

The Pinkster-flower (also called, by some, Honeysuckle, a name belonging to a quite different group) is a shrub reaching 10 feet in height. The branchlets and flower-stalks bear small stiff hairs, and the petals are hairy on the outside. Otherwise the plant is almost smooth. The flowers have little or no fragrance. The species grows in swamps or woods from Massachusetts and Vermont to South Carolina and westward to Ohio, Kentucky and Tennessee. The painting was made at Washington, D. C.

Pl. 257.　Mountain Azalea
Rhododendron roseum

This species is very similar to the Pinkster-flower, differing chiefly in being more hairy; the leaves are downy on the under side; the flower-stalks and petals are glandular and sticky; the flowers are very fragrant. It grows in woods and rocky places from Maine and Quebec to Virginia and westward to Missouri and Tennessee. The plant illustrated was grown in the greenhouses of the U. S. Department of Agriculture at Washington, D. C.

Pl. 258.　Flame Azalea
Rhododendron calendulaceum

The brilliant orange-yellow petals distinguish the Flame Azalea from most other species of North America; in some forms they are red or yellow. The plant is a shrub up to 10 feet. tall. The leaves are somewhat downy, and the flowers somewhat glandular. It grows in open woods mostly in the mountains from Pennsylvania to Georgia and Alabama and westward to West Virginia and southeastern Ohio. The plant shown was found near Linville, South Carolina.

Pl. 259.　Pink-shell Azalea
Rhododendron vaseyi

The upper petal encloses the lower ones in the bud, on which account the plant has been sometimes placed in another genus, *Blitia*. The pod opens along the sides but remains closed at the tip. It is a shrub growing up to 15 feet tall on rocky mountain slopes in acid soil. It is found only in western North Carolina, and has been so extensively gathered by nurserymen for cultivation that it is in danger of extermination. The plant illustrated grew in a garden in Washington, D. C.

Pl. 260.　Rhodora　*Rhododendron canadense*

This species also has often been placed in a separate genus on account of the irregularity of its flowers; which may be called 2-lipped. The upper lip is formed of 3 petals almost completely joined; the lower lip of 2 petals almost completely separate. There are 10 stamens.

Rhodora grows in bogs and on rocky slopes and summits from Newfoundland and Quebec to New Jersey and westward to Ontario and Pennsylvania. The plant illustrated grew at Pocono Manor, Pennsylvania.

Pl. 261.　Western Menziesia
Menziesia glabella

Menziesia is a shrub reaching a height of 10 feet. Its small red flowers have their parts in fours, with 8 stamens. The petals are joined nearly their whole length.

Western Menziesia grows in woods from Wyoming to British Columbia and southward to Oregon. The plant illustrated was gathered in the Yoho Valley near Field, British Columbia, at an altitude of 6,500 feet.

Pl. 262.　Mountain Laurel　*Kalmia latifolia*

The name Laurel has been applied to a number of unrelated plants; the Laurel with which the heroes of classical antiquity were crowned was a species of *Laurus*. The flowers of *Kalmia* hold the tips of the stamens in pockets in the petals; as the flower opens, the stamens are bent and under tension. A jar on the petals releases the stamens, which spring erect shedding their pollen. Our Mountain Laurel (when it grows in the plains it is known simply as Laurel) is a shrub which may reach a height of 30 feet and may form almost impassable thickets. The flower-stalks and sepals are glandular and sticky. It is the state flower of Connecticut.

Mountain Laurel grows in the woods from New Brunswick to Florida and westward to Ontario, Indiana and Louisiana; in spite of its name, it frequents the coastal plain. The plant illustrated grew near Washington, D. C.

[45]

Pl. 263. Bog Laurel *Kalmia polifolia*

This northern species has smooth sepals and flower-stalks. Notice that in the painting the stamens are in the "sprung" position. Bog Laurel grows in peaty soil and bogs from Labrador to Alaska and southward to Newfoundland, New England, Pennsylvania, Michigan, Minnesota, Idaho and Oregon. The western plants are sometimes placed in a separate subspecies. The specimen illustrated was grown in the greenhouses of the U. S. Department of Agriculture at Washington, D. C.

Pl. 264. Lambkill *Kalmia angustifolia*

The common name derives from the fact that the leaves of this species, as of other species of *Kalmia,* are poisonous to livestock; fortunately they are tough and unpalatable, so that they are not often grazed. Other species of this family with poisonous foliage are known in the genera *Rhododendron, Menziesia* and *Ledum.*

Lambkill grows in sterile soil, such as old pastures, from Newfoundland and Labrador to Manitoba and southward to Georgia and Tennessee. The plant illustrated grew near Washington, D. C.

Pl. 265. Small-leaved Laurel
Kalmia microphylla

This species grows only a foot high or less. Its small flowers are borne on long stalks. It inhabits moist ground from Yukon and British Columbia to Colorado and California. The painting was made from a plant collected in Burgess Pass near Field, British Columbia, at an altitude of 7,000 feet.

Pl. 266. Pink Mountain Heather
Phyllodoce empetriformis

The true Heaths and Heathers are rare and scattered in North America. This species and that shown in Plate 268 have the general aspect of the Heaths. The petals are joined to make a small vase; there are 8 to 12 stamens. The needle-like leaves are attached to the stem singly.

Phyllodoce forms a matted growth only about 18 inches high on mountain slopes near timberline from Alaska to northern California and eastward to Montana. The plant illustrated was collected in Burgess Pass near Field, British Columbia, at an altitude of 7,000 feet.

Pl. 267. Zenobia *Zenobia cassinefolia*

Zenobia is a shrub up to 10 feet tall. The flower parts are in fives. The flowers are fragrant. A closely related species is smooth and gray-green; the two species are considered one by some authors.

Zenobia cassinefolia grows in sandy soil in pine-barrens on the coastal plain from Virginia to South Carolina. The plant illustrated was collected at Rose Hill, North Carolina.

Pl. 268. Western Mountain Heather
Cassiope mertensiana

Cassiope differs from *Phyllodoce* in having scale-like leaves attached in pairs. Petals and sepals are 4 or 5, stamens 8 or 10, ovary 4- or 5-chambered. This is a creeping alpine shrub reaching a height of about a foot, growing on banks and rocky ledges from Alaska to California. The plant illustrated was found in Burgess Pass, near Field, British Columbia.

Pl. 269. Trailing Arbutus, Mayflower
Epigaea repens

Most of the flower parts of *Epigaea* are in fives. There are two leaf-like bracts beneath the sepals. There are 10 stamens which open by lengthwise clefts instead of by the pores usual in the family. The flower is very fragrant. Attempts are often made to bring this species into cultivation, almost always ending in failure, probably because it is difficult to render the soil suitable for the growth of fungi which inhabit the roots.

Trailing Arbutus inhabits sandy or peaty soil in woods from Labrador to Florida and westward to Saskatchewan, Kentucky and Louisiana. The painting was made near Washington, D. C.

Pl. 270, 271. Bearberry
Arctostaphylos uva-ursi

Arctostaphylos has about 40 species, mainly natives of the western United States. The flower parts are in fives, with 10 stamens and a 10-lobed disc around the base of the ovary. The fruit of this species is fleshy but inedible, with 5 hard nuts each containing a seed.

Bearberry is a prostrate shrub growing in sand or among rocks from Greenland to Alaska and southward to Virginia, Indiana, Illinois, New Mexico and California; also in Europe and Asia. The plant in Plate 270 was collected near Mt. Assiniboine, Alberta, at an altitude of 6,000 feet; the fruiting plant in Plate 271 near Banff, at an altitude of 4,500 feet.

Pl. 272. Ptarmigan-berry
Arctostaphylos alpina

This species is distinguished from Bearberry by its finely toothed leaves which fall in the winter. The edible fruit is in most specimens purplish-black; the painting illustrates a red-fruited form.

Ptarmigan-berry grows from Greenland and Labrador to Alaska and southward to Quebec, Maine and New Hampshire, and (the red-berried form) to Alberta and British Columbia. The plant shown came from Douglas Canyon, Alberta, at an altitude of 6,000 feet.

[46]

Wintergreen family. Pyrolaceae

Pl. 273. Pipsissewa, Prince's Pine
Chimaphila umbellata

The 5 sepals and 5 separate (or almost separate) petals, the 10 stamens and the 5-chambered ovary are characteristic of the family. The style of *Chimaphila* is very short and bears a large stigma.

Pipsissewa grows in sandy soil from Greenland to British Columbia and southward to Virginia, Ohio, Indiana, Colorado and California. The plant shown in the painting is the western variety; it was collected at Emerald Lake, near Field, British Columbia, at an altitude of 5,000 feet.

Pl. 274. One-flowered Wintergreen
Moneses uniflora

This plant resembles *Chimaphila* and *Pyrola* in general aspect; from the former it differs in having a 5-lobed stigma; from the latter in the manner in which the seed-pod splits from the top down. The stamens discharge their pollen through narrow tubes at their tips.

Moneses grows in mossy woods from Greenland to Alaska and southward to New York, Michigan, Minnesota and in the Rocky Mountains to New Mexico; also in Europe and Asia. The plant illustrated was collected on Baker Creek near Lake Louise, Alberta, at an altitude of 6,000 feet.

Pl. 275. Green Pyrola, Shinleaf
Pyrola virens

In this genus the seed-pod splits open from the base up. The flowering stalk of this species lifts its flowers about 8 or 10 inches above the ground. The tubes through which the pollen is discharged are conspicuous.

Green Pyrola grows in dry woods from Labrador to Alaska and southward to Maryland, Indiana, Wisconsin, Arizona and Oregon; also in Europe and Asia. The painting was made from a plant growing on the Siffleur River in Alberta, at an altitude of 5,000 feet.

Pl. 276. Small Pyrola, Shinleaf
Pyrola minor

The flower-stalk rises only about 6 inches high in this species. The stamens open by pores which are not lengthened into tubes. It grows in moist woods from Greenland and Labrador to Alaska and southward to New England, Michigan, Colorado and California; also in Europe and Asia. The specimen illustrated was found on the Pipestone River near Lake Louise, Alberta, at an altitude of 4,500 feet.

Pl. 277. Sidebells Pyrola Pyrola secunda

Secunda means "one-sided," and refers to the same peculiarity as the English name. The flower differs in several respects from other species of the genus: the pollen-pores are large, not tubelike; the style is long and protrudes beyond the petals; there is a 10-lobed disc around the base of the ovary. For such reasons the species has often been placed in a separate genus, *Orthilia*.

It grows in moist woods and bogs from Greenland to Alaska and southward to New England, Maryland, Indiana, Minnesota and New Mexico; also in Europe and Asia. The plant illustrated was obtained at Lake Louise, Alberta, at an altitude of 5,500 feet.

Pl. 278. Indian Pipe Monotropa uniflora

This well-known plant lacks the green color which enables most flowering plants to make their own food from materials in the soil and the air, and must live like the fungi on organic materials; for this reason it is found growing in leaf-mold under trees. There are several irregularly placed scale-like sepals (or perhaps they are bracts). The petals are thickened toward their ends. Each stamen opens by two clefts across the top.

Indian Pipe is found from Newfoundland to Washington and southward to Florida, California and Central America; also in eastern Asia. The specimen shown grew on Mt. Desert Island, Maine.

Pl. 279. Pinesap Hypopitys monotropa

Pinesap differs from Indian Pipe in having several flowers at the summit of the stem. It grows up to a foot high. Its stamens open by a single cleft which divides each head into 2 unequal halves. The plant is aromatic.

Pinesap grows in woods, mostly in acid humus, from Newfoundland to British Columbia and southward to Florida and Mexico; also in the Old World. The painting was made at Washington, D. C.

Pl. 280. Red Pinesap Hypopitys lanuginosa

This species differs from the preceding not only in its color but also in the longer style and the longer fringes of hairs on the perianth. However, intermediate plants are known, and it is possible that those authors who combine these two into one species are justified. Some authors also unite *Hypopitys* with *Monotropa*.

Red Pinesap grows in the humus of woods from Newfoundland to Florida and westward to Kentucky and Louisiana. The plant illustrated was collected near Washington, D. C.

Blueberry family. Vacciniaceae

The Blueberry Family resembles the Heaths in many ways, but the ovary is inferior, and the berry develops from the ovary and the surrounding parts of the stem-tip; the remains of the sepals may be found on the top of the berry. The flower parts are in fours or fives; the petals are joined. The plants are woody.

Pl. 281.   Box Huckleberry
Gaylussacia brachycera

The Huckleberry differs from the Blueberry (with which it is generally confused in ordinary speech) in having 10 small nutlets in the fruit; within each nutlet is a seed. The leaves of Box Huckleberry are evergreen and lack the resinous dots found on leaves of other species. The plant spreads underground, and a large clump of stems may be in reality all one plant hundreds of years old. The berries are edible but insipid.

Box Huckleberry grows in sandy woods, scattered and rather rare, from Delaware to West Virginia and Tennessee. The plant illustrated was grown in the greenhouses of the U. S. Department of Agriculture at Washington, D. C.

Pl. 282.   Deerberry
Polycodium stamineum

Polycodium is separated from the Blueberries (though not by all botanists) on the basis of rather minor characters, such as the long stalks of the flowers, the long stamens which extend beyond the petals, the pair of bristles on the stamen-head, and the small bracts—much smaller than the foliage leaves—which are associated with the flowers. This species is a shrub reaching 10 feet in height. The stamens shed their pollen through very long tubes.

Deerberry grows in dry woods from Maine to Georgia and westward to Missouri and Louisiana. The painting was made at Washington, D. C.

Pl. 283.   Highbush Blueberry
Vaccinium corymbosum

Many species of Blueberries, including this one, are the product of extensive and complicated hybridization in nature, as a result of which highly variable populations are formed which can scarcely be assigned to definite species. In general *Vaccinium corymbosum* is a name given to Blueberries which grow to heights of 15 feet, and form blue or almost black fruits; their leaves are often finely toothed and nearly smooth underneath.

They grow in swamps, wet woods, or upland woods from Nova Scotia and Quebec to Wisconsin and southward to New Jersey, Ohio and Indiana. The plant illustrated was grown in the greenhouses of the U. S. Department of Agriculture at Washington, D. C.

Pl. 284.   Pineland Blueberry
Vaccinium tenellum

This is a shrub growing as high as 12 feet and often spreading underground to form large patches. The leaves are usually broader near the tip than at the base and finely toothed. The petals vary from pink to red. The berries are small and black.

Vaccinium tenellum grows in sandy places on the

coastal plain from Virginia to Georgia. The painting was made at Beaufort, South Carolina.

Pl. 285, 286.   Mountain Cranberry, Cowberry
Vaccinium vitis-idaea

This is a creeping evergreen shrub, its leaves thick, pale and dotted with black on the under side. The flower parts are in fours, with 8 stamens. The red berry is edible.

Mountain Cranberry grows in rocky places in the woods from Greenland to Alaska and southward to New England, Minnesota, Alberta and British Columbia. Our plants are classified in a separate variety from those of Europe and Asia. The flowering plant illustrated was gathered at Lake Louise, Alberta, at an altitude of 5,500 feet; the fruiting plant on the Siffleur River, Alberta, at 4,000 feet.

Diapensia family.
Diapensiaceae

Pl. 287.   Oconee-bells   *Shortia galacifolia*

Members of the Diapensia Family are much like the Heaths, having flower parts in fives, except that the ovary has 3 compartments; the petals are joined at the base. In *Shortia* there are 5 stamens and between them 5 scales which are rudiments of stamens; the stalks of the stamens are joined with the lower parts of the petals.

Oconee-bells is rather rare; it grows in ravines and on banks in humus in the Piedmont and Blue Ridge regions of North and South Carolina. The plant illustrated was grown in the greenhouses of the U. S. Department of Agriculture at Washington, D. C.

Pl. 288.   Pyxie   *Pyxidanthera barbulata*

This species makes mats a yard or so across, formed of creeping stems bearing needle-like leaves and covered with stalkless flowers. The petals vary from rose to white. The stamens are joined to the petals. Their heads open by a lid, like a box; the name of the genus is derived from the Greek word for a box; the English name is simply the Anglicizing of the same word.

Pyxie grows in the pine barrens, in sandy soil, from New Jersey to South Carolina. The plants shown were collected at Whitesbog, New Jersey.

Primrose family.
Primulaceae

The Primrose Family is known by having 5 petals united at least at their bases and 5 stamens attached to the petals and situated opposite to them (rather than opposite to the gaps between them); the pistil is not divided into compartments; the numerous ovules are attached to a small knob which rises from the base of the cavity.

Pl. 289. Pigmy Androsace
Androsace subumbellata

The basal rosettes of leaves are well shown in the painting of this tiny species. It is an annual, and grows in stony soil from Hudson Bay to British Columbia and southward in the mountains to Colorado and Arizona. The plants shown came from the headwaters of Johnson Creek, Alberta, at an altitude of 7,500 feet.

Pl. 290. Sweet Androsace
Androsace carinata

The species of *Androsace* are most numerous in Asia; they are mostly plants of the far north. They are like Primroses with much shorter petal-tubes and styles. *Androsace carinata* is perennial, sending up a flower-stalk about 2 inches high. The flower-stalk is white wt hhair and the leaves are fringed with hairs. The petals are white or yellowish with a yellow center.

This species grows in the high mountains from Colorado and Utah to Alberta. The painting was made from a plant found in Ptarmigan Pass, near Lake Louise, Alberta, at an altitude of 7,500 feet.

Pl. 291. Bird's-eye Primrose
Primula mistassinica

Most of the species of *Primula* inhabit the mountains of Asia. The leaves in our species are basal, the flowers in an umbel (a cluster with stalks radiating from one point like the ribs of an umbrella). The petals are joined in a definite tube, from which their upper parts spread out in 5 lobes. There are 5 stamens attached to the petal-tube and opposite the lobes. In this species the flower-stalk rises a foot above the ground; the notched or cleft petal-lobes vary from pink to purple or white. The flower resembles that of a Pink (see Plate 101), but in the Pink Family the petals are separate.

This Primrose is found here and there on rocks and banks from Greenland to Alberta and southward to New England, New York, Michigan, Illinois, Minnesota and Nevada. The plant illustrated was collected at Bow Lake north of Lake Louise, Alberta, at an altitude of 5,000 feet.

Pl. 292. Shooting-star
Dodecatheon meadia

The sharply reflexed petals of Shooting-star suggest the flower of Cyclamen, which is also a member of this family. They vary in color from white to pink and lilac. The stamens are joined together at their bases; their heads form a cone which surrounds the stigma. The flower-stalk rises to as much as 18 inches above the ground.

Shooting-star grows in prairies and meadows and in open woods from Virginia to Georgia and westward to Missouri and Texas. The painting was made at Washington, D. C.

Pl. 293. Slender Shooting-star
Dodecatheon pauciflorum

This species has a flower-stalk up to a foot high, but the flowers are considerably smaller and fewer than those of the eastern Shooting-star. It occurs in wet meadows from Saskatchewan to British Columbia and southward to Colorado and Washington. The plant in the painting was found near Lake Louise at an altitude of 5,500 feet.

Olive family. Oleaceae

Pl. 294. Fringe-tree
Chionanthus virginiana

Fringe-tree is much grown for ornament. The 4 very narrow petals are separate almost to the base; there are 2 stamens attached to the petals; and a 2-chambered ovary. The fruit resembles a berry but contains a stone, within which are the seeds. Other members of this family are Lilac, Forsythia, Privet, Jasmine, Ash and Olive.

Fringe-tree is found along streams in woods from New Jersey to Florida and westward to Ohio, Missouri and Texas. The branch shown was collected near Washington, D. C.

Logania family. Loganiaceae

Pl. 295. Carolina Jessamine
Gelsemium sempervirens

Several different shrubs and vines with fragrant flowers, in different families, have been called Jessamine or Jasmine. Carolina Jessamine is a vine with leaves in pairs. Its flowers have 5 united petals, 5 stamens joined with the petals at their base, and a 2-chambered ovary; the style bears 4 narrow stigmas. The fruit is a flattish pod.

Gelsemium sempervirens grows in woods from Virginia to Florida and westward to Arkansas, Texas and Mexico. The painting was made from a branch taken near Beaufort, South Carolina.

Gentian family. Gentianaceae

GENTIAN *GENTIANA*

The Gentian Family has parts in fives, with the petals joined into a tube, and an ovary with ovules on the inner surface of the single cavity, sometimes arranged in 2 groups or lines. The petals of the Gentians are twisted in the bud rather than merely overlapping or just meeting at the edges; the stamens are attached to the petals. Many species have folded appendages at the notches between the free, spreading parts of the petals.

Pl. 296. Felwort *Gentiana amarella*

This Gentian may grow nearly 2 feet high. The small petals vary in color from cream-colored to violet or lilac. At the top of the petal-tube, where the 5 separate lobes diverge, is a fringe of hair-like bodies. The flowers grow in clusters from the same points as the leaves.

Felwort grows on wet rocks, gravel or sand, or in damp grass, from Labrador to Alaska and southward to New England, Minnesota, South Dakota, New Mexico, California and Mexico; also in Europe and Asia. As one would expect from such a range, the species consists of many varieties. The plant illustrated was found near Lake Louise, Alberta, at an altitude of 5,000 feet.

Pl. 297. Fringed Gentian
Gentiana crinita

There are several Gentians with fringed petals, of which *Gentiana crinita* is the best known, at least in the eastern states. It grows nearly 3 feet high, with a single flower at the end of each stem. A curious feature of its distribution is that the plants disappear entirely from a certain region, springing up somewhere else; perhaps because the tiny seeds all blow away or fail to germinate easily. The species is found rather locally, therefore, in low woods and wet meadows from Maine to Georgia and westward to Manitoba, Iowa and Pennsylvania. The plant illustrated was collected near Mt. Kisco, New York.

Pl. 298. Pine-barren Gentian
Gentiana porphyrio

This species may grow to be 18 inches tall. The flowers grow singly at the tips of the stems. The tube of united petals bears, in the notches between its 5 pointed lobes, 5 fringed appendages. *Gentiana porphyrio* grows in moist places in pine barrens on the coastal plain from New Jersey to South Carolina. The plant illustrated came from Wilmington, North Carolina.

Pl. 299. Bottle Gentian, Soapwort
Gentiana saponaria

The species is named from the resemblance of its foliage to the common Bouncing Bet, *Saponaria,* in the Pink Family, and not because it is one of the several plants which yield a soap-like, suds-forming substance. It is a tall plant, reaching a height of 3 feet, bearing its large flowers in a terminal cluster. The petals vary in color from white to blue. It grows in bogs and swamps, mostly in sandy soil, on the coastal plain from New York to Georgia and Louisiana, and less commonly inland to Minnesota and Texas. The plant shown was collected near Washington, D. C.

Pl. 300. Ruff Gentian *Gentiana calycosa*

This small species grows to a foot or so high, bearing a few large flowers at the tip. The lobes of the joined petals alternate with smaller appendages in the notches. The species grows in alpine meadows high in the mountains from Montana to Washington and southward to Wyoming and California. The specimen illustrated was found in Indian Pass in Glacier National Park, Montana, at an altitude of 6,500 feet.

Pl. 301. Prairie Gentian *Gentiana affinis*

Prairie Gentian grows to a height of 18 inches, forming a number of flowers in a long cluster. The petal-tube is rather narrow and bears at its rim not only the 5 separate petal-lobes but, in the notches between them, 5 fringed appendages almost as large, so that one may think that there are 10 petals present. The species is found in damp soil and prairies from Minnesota to British Columbia and southward to Colorado, Utah, Idaho and Nevada; similar plants in Oregon and California are often classified as a variety of the same species. The painting was made from plants collected on Red Deer River, Alberta, at an altitude of 5,500 feet.

Pl. 302. Blue-green Gentian
Gentiana glauca

The Blue-green Gentian is typical of the many truly alpine and arctic species which grow only a few inches above the ground; many species have pale blue or even green flowers. This species is found from Montana to Alaska and southward to Alberta and British Columbia; also in eastern Asia, the home of many species of Gentians. The plant illustrated was collected in Ptarmigan Pass near Lake Louise, at an altitude of 7,500 feet.

Pl. 303. Salt-marsh Rose-gentian
Sabbatia stellaris

Sabbatia is distinguished from *Gentiana* by its pink petals which are joined only at the base to form a very short tube; the style is cleft in two.

Sabbatia stellaris inhabits brackish marshes along the coast from Massachusetts to Florida and Louisiana and more rarely inland to Indiana and Kentucky, as well as the West Indies. The plant shown in the painting was found near Bridgeport, Connecticut.

Pl. 304. Pink Centaury
Centaurium venustum

A peculiarity of Centaury is the 2 fan-shaped stigmas at the tip of the long style. The pink petals are joined only at the base so that there is scarcely any tube of petals.

Pink Centaury grows only in southern California, although it has relatives in other parts of the United States. The plant illustrated was collected at Torrey Pines near La Jolla, California.

[50]

Pl. 305. Bogbean, Buckbean
Menyanthes trifoliata

Bogbean sends up its leaves from a thick creeping stem which grows in mud or boggy peat often under water. Each leaf stalk bears 3 leaflets. The petals are white, often with the reflexed tips tinged with pink; the inner surface is bearded. For various reasons, such as the arrangement of the petals in the bud, *Menyanthes* is often placed in a separate family.

Bogbean grows in bogs and swamps from Labrador to Alaska and southward to Virginia, Ohio, Missouri, Nebraska, Colorado and California. The plant illustrated was collected in a bog near Lake Louise, Alberta, at an altitude of 5,500 feet.

Milkweed family. Asclepiadaceae

Pl. 306. Showy Milkweed
Asclepias speciosa

The Milkweeds have a very complex flower. There are 5 sepals and 5 petals, all reflexed; just above the petals is a corona (crown) of 5 upright tubular or scoop-shaped bodies colored like petals, each bearing a curved horn; these are often the most conspicuous parts of the flower. The heads of the 5 stamens cohere, and also adhere to the large stigma; the pollen of each pollen sack forms one large waxy mass and is so disposed that an insect which alights on the stigma becomes entangled with the pollen and carries away 2 of the pollen-masses on its leg — to be deposited on the stigma of the next flower visited. The pistil grows into a large pod which splits open along one side and reveals numerous seeds which bear tufts of long silky hairs.

Asclepias speciosa grows up to 6 feet tall. The flower-stalks, the under side of the leaves and the pods are coated with fine white wool. It grows on prairies and in woodland openings from Manitoba and Minnesota to British Columbia and southward to Missouri, Texas, New Mexico, Arizona and California. The painting was made from a plant gathered at Fairmount Hot Springs, British Columbia, at an altitude of 3,000 feet.

Pl. 307. Butterfly-weed
Asclepias tuberosa

Asclepias was dedicated to the Greek god of healing, whose name is usually Latinized as Aesculapius. Its species do not, however, seem to have been used medicinally; they are poisonous to livestock.

Butterfly-weed is so called from the butterflies which are almost always to be seen on its flowers. The yellow or orange flowers and the lack of milky juice distinguish it from other milkweeds. The species is variable and has been separated into several varieties. It grows

on prairies and in meadows and sandy places from Maine to Florida and westward to Minnesota, Colorado, Mississippi and Arizona. The specimen illustrated was collected near Washington, D. C.

Phlox family. Polemoniaceae

Pl. 308. Wild Sweet William
Phlox divaricata

The resemblance between *Phlox* and the garden Sweet William is superficial; the latter has separate petals, while those of *Phlox* are joined to form a tube, with the lobes flaring at right angles. The 5 stamens are attached at different levels on the tube. The pistil is divided into 3 and the style is 3-cleft with 3 stigmas. The petals of *Phlox divaricata* vary in color from white to pink, lavender or blue. The flower-stalks and sepals bear fine glandular hairs. Its flowering stem grows from a stem which creeps at the surface of the ground.

Phlox divaricata is found in open woods and meadows from Quebec and Vermont to Georgia, mostly west of the coastal plain, and westward to Minnesota and Texas. Plants of the more westerly regions are classed in a separate variety. Several forms, mostly dwarfish, are common in cultivation. The plant illustrated came from Plummer's Island in the Potomac River, a locality known for the intrusion of midwestern species.

Pl. 309. Jacob's Ladder, Greek Valerian
Polemonium reptans

Polemonium differs from *Phlox* in having the long leaves divided into many narrow leaflets. The joined petals form a bell instead of a tube.

Jacob's Ladder grows in rich woods from New York to Virginia and westward to Minnesota, Missouri and Alabama. It is often cultivated.

Fouquieria family. Fouquieriaceae

Pl. 310. Ocotillo *Fouquieria splendens*

Ocotillo is a shrub composed of unbranched stems sometimes 15 feet long and covered with spines; the spines are derived from leaf stalks which have lost their leaves; in the angle between spine and stem a bunch of secondary leaves appears. The 5 petals form a tube from which the 10 or more stamens project; the pistil is more or less divided into 3 parts.

Ocotillo grows on mesas in the deserts from Texas to southern California and southward into northern Mexico. The plant illustrated was collected near Superior, Arizona.

Waterleaf family. Hydrophyllaceae

Pl. 311. Sand Phacelia *Phacelia linearis*

The Phacelias differ from the Phlox Family chiefly in the ovary, which has only one cavity, and which bears a style cleft in 2 instead of 3 branches. The group is a large one, especially in the western United States; the species differ only slightly. *Phacelia linearis* is somewhat hairy; the leaves are cut into narrow lobes. The petals vary from white to blue or purple.

The species grows in rocky and sandy places from Wyoming to British Columbia and southward to Utah and California. The painting shows a plant found near Radium Hot Springs, British Columbia, at an altitude of 2,500 feet.

Pl. 312. Silky Phacelia *Phacelia sericea*

Sericea means "silky"; the finely cleft leaves of *Phacelia sericea* are covered with gray silky hairs. The alpine character of this species is further shown by the massive root which bears a low stem. The flowers are crowded; they vary in color from white to bluish-purple.

Phacelia sericea grows on high rocky slopes from Colorado to British Columbia and southward to California and Nevada. The painting was made from a plant gathered at Glacier, British Columbia, at an altitude of 6,500 feet.

Pl. 313. Mistmaiden
Romanzoffia sitchensis

Romanzoffia differs from the other members of the family in having an undivided style; the fruit, however, is more or less divided into 2 chambers. The bases of the leaf stalks are dilated in this species and overlap to form a sort of bulb.

Romanzoffia sitchensis grows on wet rocks high in the mountains from Alaska to California and eastward to Alberta and Montana. The plant shown was found at Lake O'Hara, British Columbia, at an altitude of 6,600 feet.

Borage family. Boraginaceae

The Borage Family has its parts in fives except for the ovary, which is usually 4-lobed. The petals are joined so as to make a more or less tubular part and a flaring part; where the lower part ends there are often 5 small scales which may almost close the mouth of the tube. As the ovary becomes the fruit, the 4 lobes separate into 4 one-seeded nuts.

[52]

Pl. 314. Bluebell, Virginia Cowslip
Mertensia virginica

The bell formed by the petals is narrow below (the tube) and flares into an upper part which is indented on the sides. As the painting shows, the petals are pink in the bud and become blue as they grow older. This plant should not be confused with the Bluebells of Scotland (*Campanula;* it grows also all over northern Europe and North America) or with English Bluebells (*Scilla*); and true Cowslip is a *Primula* with yellow flowers.

Mertensia virginica grows in open woods and bottom-lands from New York to South Carolina and westward to Minnesota, Kansas and Alabama. It is often cultivated. The painting was made at Washington, D. C.

Pl. 315. Tall Lungwort
Mertensia paniculata

This species is more or less hairy. It may reach a height of 2 feet. As the painting shows, the style is long, the stamens short. The petals bear conspicuous crests at the end of the tubular part.

Tall Lungwort grows in moist woods and meadows from Quebec to Alaska and southward to Michigan, Wisconsin, Iowa, Montana, Idaho and Oregon. The plant shown was found on Lake Minnewonka near Banff, Alberta, at an altitude of 4,000 feet.

Pl. 316. Moss Forget-me-not
Eritrichium elongatum

This plant forms a moss-like cushion with leaves only about ¼ inch long. The distinction between this genus and the true Forget-me-not lies in minute technical characteristics, such as the manner of attachment of the 4 nutlets which compose the fruit.

Moss Forget-me-not grows on rocky ridges high in the mountains from Wyoming and Colorado to eastern Oregon. The specimen illustrated came from Yellowstone National Park, Montana.

Pl. 317. Bur Forget-me-not
Lappula diffusa

The nutlets of this genus bear minute barbed bristles, for which reason it is often called Stickseed. This species forms spreading branches up to 2 feet long. The petals are joined only at the base, and where they spread apart bear a prominent crest; they vary from white to blue.

Lappula diffusa grows on moist rocks and cliffs from British Columbia to Oregon and eastward to Wyoming and Utah. The painting was made at Lake Louise, Alberta, from a plant growing at an altitude of 5,000 feet.

Pl. 318. Alpine Forget-me-not
Myosotis alpestris

Myosotis includes the familiar species called Forget-me-not which are found growing in moist places; many of them are cultivated. *Myosotis alpestris* is a perennial. The leaves and stem are hairy; most of the leaves grow from the base of the stem. It is found in wet places in the mountains from Colorado to Alaska; also in Europe and Asia. The plant illustrated was gathered at Baker Lake near Lake Louise, Alberta, at an altitude of 6,500 feet.

Verbena family. Verbenaceae

Pl. 319. Verbena *Verbena canadensis*

Verbena canadensis is a spreading plant, its branches tending to lie on the ground with their ends ascending. The leaves vary greatly in the depth of their lobes or teeth. The whole plant is more or less hairy. The flowers are slightly irregular, the spreading part of the petals being a little larger on one side than on the other; the petals vary from white to rose, lilac or blue, and change in color somewhat with age. There are 4 stamens, 2 shorter than the other 2. The ovary is somewhat 4-lobed and in fruit becomes 4 small one-seeded nuts.

This species of *Verbena* grows on rocky ledges and in sandy soil from Virginia to Florida and westward to Colorado and Texas. To call it Canada Verbena would strain our notions of geography; but when the epithet *canadensis* was given to it, Canada extended over most of North America west of the Mississippi River.

Pl. 320. French Mulberry, Beautyberry *Callicarpa americana*

This is a shrub which grows to a height of 10 feet. The branchlets and the under sides of the leaves are densely woolly with branched hairs. The flowers are small, in dense clusters, and vary from white to pink or blue; each has 4 petals and 4 equal stamens. The ovary becomes the "berry"; this contains 4 stones inside each of which is a seed.

Callicarpa americana grows in moist woods, thickets and bottom lands from Maryland to Florida, westward to Texas and northward into Tennessee, Arkansas and Oklahoma and southward into northern Mexico; also in the West Indies and Bermuda. It is widely cultivated.

Mint family. Labiatae

Pl. 321. Skullcap *Scutellaria serrata*

The Mint Family resembles the two preceding families in having a 4-lobed ovary. It is distinguished by its usually bilabiate (2-lipped) flower; the lips are formed by the union of 5 petals of unequal size. This is well seen in the painting of Skullcap: the upper lip is composed of 1 hooded petal; there are 2 smaller petal-lobes at the sides; and a spreading lower lip notched at the end and probably composed of 2 petals. There are 4 stamens. There are many species of this genus; *Scutellaria serrata* is known by the size and shape of its leaves, which are smooth or very nearly so. As in most plants of this family, the stems are square.

Scutellaria serrata grows in woods from New York to Georgia and westward to Ohio, Missouri and Alabama. The plant illustrated was found near Washington, D. C.

Pl. 322. Horsemint *Monarda punctata*

This Horsemint (the name is applied also to other species) may reach a height of over 3 feet. Its flowers grow in whorls partly concealed by the special leaves called bracts; these are tinged with color at the base, the color varying from white to lilac or reddish. The petals are yellowish spotted with purple and form an upper lip which is very long and curved; the 2 stamens and the 2-cleft style follow the arch of this upper lip.

Monarda punctata is found chiefly in sandy places from New Jersey to Florida and Texas, and northward to Michigan, Minnesota and Kansas; the midwestern plants are classified in distinct subspecies or varieties characterized by differences in the hairiness of the plants. The painting was made at Washington, D. C.

Pl. 323. Beebalm, Oswego Tea *Monarda didyma*

The flowers in this species have the same structure as in the preceding, but the petals are a bright red and the bracts also are often tinged with red; the flowers are clustered at the summit of the stem, which may reach a height of 5 feet. The flowers are frequented by hummingbirds as well as by bees.

Beebalm grows in rich woods and bottom lands from New York to Michigan and southward in the mountains to Georgia. It is widely cultivated, and the cultivated varieties include some with pink flowers.

Figwort family. Scrophulariaceae

The Figwort Family is known by its irregular and usually 2-lipped flower, the petals being joined, its 4 stamens in 2 sizes, and its 2-chambered ovary which becomes a pod usually containing many seeds. It includes perhaps 4,000 species, among which we may recognize Snapdragon and Foxglove in addition to those described below.

MONKEY-FLOWER *MIMULUS*

The genus *Mimulus* contains nearly 100 species, mostly in western North America, all generally known as Monkey-flower. The petals of many species seem to make a sort of face; hence the name *Mimulus,* which means a mimic, an actor, a buffoon. The genus is known by the 5-angled tube made by the joined sepals. The petals form a tube which is 2-lipped at the end, the upper lip of 2 lobes, the lower of 3. The lower lip bears also 2 ridges which almost close the opening of the tube. Most of the species frequent wet places.

Pl. 324.   Monkey-flower   *Mimulus guttatus*
Mimulus guttatus is highly variable in details and is classified into several varieties or subspecies. It is smooth except for the flower-stalks, which are very finely glandular. It grows by streams and in other wet places from Alaska to Baja California and eastward to South Dakota, Colorado, New Mexico and Chihuahua. The plant shown in the painting was gathered near Vancouver, British Columbia.

Pl. 325.   Scarlet Monkey-flower
Mimulus cardinalis
The painting shows the long flower-stalks; also the long style with its 2 stigmas, which lasts until after the petals and stamens have fallen. The sepals also hang on, forming a cup around the base of the ovary.
Scarlet Monkey-flower frequents the banks of streams from Oregon to Arizona and Baja California. The plant illustrated was found near a spring in the Grand Canyon of the Colorado River in Arizona.

Pl. 326.   Lewis' Monkey-flower
Mimulus lewisii
This species may reach a height of 3 feet. Its dull red flowers are on stalks that may be 4 inches long, as is evident in the painting. The species was named for Meriwether Lewis, the famous explorer of western America. It grows on wet banks from Alaska to California and eastward to Montana and Colorado. The specimen illustrated was collected near Glacier, British Columbia, at an altitude of 3,500 feet.

Pl. 327.   Alpine Monkey-flower
Mimulus caespitosus
This alpine species grows only about 4 inches high. The 2 ridges in the lower lip are particularly well developed, almost forming what in other genera is called a palate. *Mimulus caespitosus* is found along streams and in crevices of wet rocks in the Selkirk Mountains of British Columbia and the Cascade and Olympic Mountains of Washington. The painting was made from a plant gathered in the Asulkan Valley near Glacier, British Columbia, at an altitude of 3,500 feet.

Pl. 328.   Bush Monkey-flower
Diplacus longiflorus
The genus *Diplacus* is closely related to *Mimulus* and is included in it by some botanists. It differs in being woody, in being generally hairy with branched hairs, and in the manner of the opening of the pod.

[54]

This species grows to about 3 feet high. It is sticky as well as hairy. The short flower-stalks may be compared with those of the preceding species of *Mimulus.*
Diplacus longiflorus grows mostly in the chaparral in the foothills of the mountains of California and Baja California, at altitudes up to 5,000 feet. The specimen illustrated was found near Los Angeles.

Pl. 329.   Red Monkey-flower
Diplacus puniceus
This highly variable species has many branches and may reach a height of 5 feet. It is sticky throughout and the leaves bear star-like (stellate) hairs on the lower surface. It grows in the chaparral on dry hillsides in California and Baja California. The plant shown was gathered near Torrey Pines.

Pl. 330.   Turtlehead   *Chelone glabra*
Turtlehead is named from its petals, the arrangement of which is sufficient for recognition. They are joined to form a tube which spreads into 2 lips; the upper, hooded lip is notched and probably consists of 2 petals, the lower lip 3-lobed, with the middle lobe the shortest; the floor of the lower lip is elevated into a woolly palate which almost closes the entrance to the tube. There are 4 good stamens and a rudiment of a fifth; the fertile stamens are woolly, the sterile one green and smooth. The sepals are unusual in not being joined.
Turtlehead grows in wet ground and along streams from Newfoundland to Minnesota and southward to Georgia, Alabama and Missouri. The painting was made on Mt. Desert Island, Maine.

BEARD-TONGUE   *PENSTEMON*

The name *Penstemon* is an abbreviation of *Pentastemon,* from the Greek words meaning "five stamens." Most members of the Figwort Family have only 4 stamens; and even in this genus the fifth is sterile, forms no pollen. The "bearded tongue" is this same fifth stamen, which is hairy in many species. The petals are joined to form a tube; the 5 lobes at the end form 2 more or less distinct lips, 2 lobes in the upper lips and 3 in the lower; there are usually 2 ridges in the lower lip. The leaves are in pairs, the flowers in a loose cluster toward the top. It is a large genus, having more than 200 species which are often very difficult to determine; most of them grow in western America. Many species are in cultivation.

Pl. 331.   Foxglove Penstemon
Penstemon digitalis
One of the flowers in the painting is so disposed that one can see the 4 fertile stamens within the petal-tube; their stalks curve in a characteristic manner. The flowers have little evidence of the 2 lips. The plant reaches a height of 5 feet; it is smooth and glossy, with a gray-green tint.

Penstemon digitalis grows in open woodlands and prairies from Maine to South Dakota and southward to Alabama, Kansas and Texas. It is also cultivated. The plant shown was obtained near Washington, D. C.

Pl. 332. Prairie Beard-tongue
Penstemon eriantherus

This species grows to a height of only about a foot. The plant is more or less hairy and sticky. The petals vary in color from pale lilac to pinkish or blue, with purple lines. The sterile stamen is long and bears a yellow beard.

Penstemon eriantherus grows in dry soil from North and South Dakota to Washington and northward to Alberta and British Columbia. The plant illustrated was collected near Sinclair Hot Springs, British Columbia, at an altitude of 2,500 feet.

Pl. 333. Fire Penstemon
Penstemon eatoni

The Fire Penstemon is distinguished from other species by its narrow tapering petal-tube which bears short lobes. It may reach a height of 2 feet. It grows in dry soils from Utah to New Mexico and westward to California. The painting was made from a plant found near Superior, Arizona.

Pl. 334. Lyall's Penstemon
Penstemon lyallii

Lyall's Penstemon is another smooth species, growing to a height of a foot or so; the sepals are hairy and somewhat sticky. It is found in the mountains from Montana to Idaho and northward into Alberta and British Columbia. The specimen shown was gathered in Sinclair Canyon near Radium Hot Springs, British Columbia, at an altitude of 3,000 feet.

Pl. 335. Rock Penstemon
Penstemon rupicola

This species rises only 4 inches or less from the ground, forming a mat. The gray-green leaves are roundish and very thick. The 2-lipped character of the petals is clearly shown in the painting. The sterile stamen is short. The Rock Penstemon grows in crevices from Washington to northern California. The plant illustrated was collected near Paradise Valley on Mount Rainier, Washington.

Pl. 336. Desert Penstemon
Penstemon parryi

Penstemon parryi is smooth, gray-green, and grows to a height of 2 feet. The flower is scarcely 2-lipped. The species is found in canyons and on mountain slopes in southern Arizona and northern Sonora. It is closely related to other species which range into Texas and California, and perhaps these are all parts of one species. The specimen shown was gathered on Tumamoc Hill near Tucson, Arizona.

Pl. 337. Blue-eyed Mary
Collinsia verna

Blue-eyed Mary grows only about 6 inches high. The flowers are evidently 2-lipped, the 2 upper petals being different in color from the 3 lower; the middle lobe of the lower lip is folded around the stamens and style. The fifth stamen is present, as in *Penstemon*, but reduced to a sort of gland.

Blue-eyed Mary is found along streams and in moist woods from New York to Wisconsin and southward and westward to Kentucky and Missouri. The painting was made from a plant grown in a garden in Washington, D. C.

Pl. 338. Butter-and-eggs, Toadflax
Linaria vulgaris

This plant, though a native of Europe, has become a weed in America. The lowest petal bears a spur (in abnormal specimens all 5 petals are spurred). The palate of darker yellow nearly closes the throat of the petal-tube. Only long-tongued bees can penetrate this flower and reach the nectar in the spur; in doing so they transfer the pollen; the palate prevents pilfering by smaller insects.

Toadflax grows in pastures, roadsides and cultivated ground throughout almost all of the United States and the southern parts of Canada.

Pl. 339. False Foxglove
Aureolaria virginica

The 5 petals are joined for most of their length and then flare into 5 lobes which are almost equal in size. The 4 stamens are in 2 lengths. The stalks of the stamens and the inner surface of the petals are woolly; the plant itself is smooth. It may reach a height of 6 feet.

Aureolaria virginica is found in dry open woods where it is parasitic upon the roots of oaks, drawing at least part of its nourishment from them. It ranges from New Hampshire to Michigan and southward to Florida and Louisiana.

Pl. 340. Red Helmet
Pedicularis bracteosa

The name of the genus is derived from the Latin for louse, and the species are often called Lousewort. There is an old superstition that the eating of these plants by livestock would engender lice. The species are characterized by the strongly 2-lipped structure of the joined petals; the upper lip is concave and arched and sometimes prolonged into a beak. There are 4 stamens in 2 sizes. *Pedicularis bracteosa* varies in the color of its petals; they may be yellowish or purple. There are 5 joined sepals, the uppermost much shorter than the others. The flowering stem grows up to 3 feet high.

Red Helmet grows in sandy and rocky places in coniferous forests from Montana to Alberta, Idaho and eastern Washington. The plant illustrated was found at Baker Lake near Lake Louise, Alberta, at an altitude of 6,000 feet.

[55]

Pl. 341.   Alpine Fern-Leaf
Pedicularis contorta
The petals vary from white to yellow and are marked with purple. The upper lip curves up at the extreme tip; it is enfolded by the lower lip. The upper sepal is shorter than the others. The plant reaches a height of 2 feet.

Pedicularis contorta grows in mountain meadows and openings in coniferous forests from Montana to British Columbia and southward to northern California. The plant shown was collected on Mt. St. Piran near Lake Louise, Alberta, at an altitude of 7,000 feet.

Pl. 342.   Elephant-head
Pedicularis groenlandica
This species is characterized by the long upcurving beak on the end of the upper lip of the flower, from which it gets its common name. It has often been placed in a separate genus, *Elephantella*. The 5 sepals are of equal length. The plant grows to a height of 2 feet or more.

Elephant-head occurs in moist mountain meadows from Greenland and Labrador to Alaska and southward to New Mexico in the Rocky Mountains and to California in the Sierra Nevadas. The specimen sketched was found in Ptarmigan Valley near Lake Louise, at an altitude of 6,000 feet.

Pl. 343.   Owl Clover
Orthocarpus tenuifolius
The conspicuous colored parts of Owl Clover are not flowers but bracts, special leaves associated with the flowers which more or less conceal them. The flowers themslves have a tube of yellow petals 2-lipped at the end. There are 4 lobes or teeth to the cup formed by the joined sepals. The plant rises about 8 inches above the ground. It is more or less hairy. *Orthocarpus* is closely related to *Castilleia* (see below), but differs in the lower lip of its petals, which is as long as the upper lip and 3-lobed.

Owl Clover, which is no relation to true Clover (*Trifolium* in the Leguminosae) grows on the plains from Idaho to Washington and British Columbia. The plant illustrated came from Cranbrook, British Columbia.

Pl. 344.   Indian Paintbrush
Castilleia miniata
As in *Orthocarpus,* the colored parts are mainly the bracts, in this species red and often 3-lobed. The flowers arise in the angles between bracts and stem; the petals are joined to make a tube; they are green with narrow red edges. The tube is 2-lipped at the end, the lower lip much shorter than the upper. This species of Indian Paintbrush (there are many) varies greatly in all these characteristics. It grows to a height of 2 feet.

Castilleia miniata is found in meadows or openings in coniferous forests from Montana to Washington and British Columbia and southward to Colorado and California. The painting shows a plant gathered on the headwaters of the Clearwater River in Alberta, at an altitude of 6,500 feet.

Pl. 345.   Pale Paintbrush
Castilleia pallida
This arctic species grows to a height of 18 inches. It is more or less hairy. The bracts vary in color from almost white to pale yellow and to various shades of pale rose. Pale Paintbrush grows from Alaska southward and eastward to Alberta and British Columbia. The painting was made on the Clearwater River in Alberta, at an altitude of 8,000 feet.

Pl. 346.   Lance-leaf Paintbrush
Castilleia lancifolia
The Lance-leaf Paintbrush grows 2 feet high. Its petals are green with crimson edges; the sepals are hairy. The bracts are scarlet and are noticeably hairy at the base — a characteristic evident in the painting. The species grows in valleys and on hillsides from Alaska southward and eastward to Colorado, Utah, Alberta and Oregon. The specimen illustrated came from the Pipestone River, near Lake Louise, Alberta, at an altitude of 5,500 feet.

Bladderwort family.
Lentibulariaceae

Pl. 347.   Butterwort
Pinguicula vulgaris
Butterwort is sometimes confused with the Violets; but the 5 petals are united, there are only 2 stamens, and the stigma is borne on a very short style. The name is derived from the buttery or greasy appearance of the leaves (the Latin *pinguis* also means "fat"). These leaves, which have a fungus-like odor, are covered with small glands sticky enough to catch minute insects; digestive juices are also exuded, so that the plant is actually carnivorous like the Pitcher-plants. Another genus in this family is *Utricularia*, Bladderwort, which grows in water and entraps small animals in its bladders.

Butterwort grows only a few inches high; it is found on wet rocks and banks and in bogs from Labrador to Alaska and southward to New England, New York, Michigan, Minnesota and Washington. The plant shown grew on the Bow River near Banff, British Columbia, at an altitude of 4,000 feet.

Pl. 348.   Southern Butterwort
Pinguicula elatior
This species may grow a foot high; the flower-stalk bears white hairs at the base. It grows in pinelands on the coastal plain from North Carolina to Florida. The plant shown was grown in the greenhouses of the U. S. Department of Agriculture at Washington, D. C.

Broom-rape family. Orobanchaceae

Pl. 349. Cancer-root *Orobanche uniflora*

Cancer-root is so called because it is attached under the ground to the roots of other plants, such as Golden-rod, and draws its food from them. Because of its lack of green pigment it is unable to make its own food. Each stem, which rises only 2 or 3 inches above the ground, bears a single flower. The petals are joined to form a slightly curved tube which flares at the end into 5 almost equal lobes; the color varies from white to light pink or lavender. There are 4 stamens, 2 longer than the other 2; the ovary is 1-chambered.

Cancer-root grows in woods and on banks from Newfoundland and Quebec to British Columbia and southward to Florida, Texas and California. The plants illustrated were gathered on Plummer's Island in the Potomac River.

Pl. 350. Squaw-root
Conopholis americana

Conopholis is parasitic on several kinds of trees. It differs from *Orobanche* in having 2 lips at the end of the tube of joined petals; this structure is seen in the painting. The numerous scales on the stem are the leaves.

Squaw-root is found in rich woods from Nova Scotia to Michigan and southward to Florida and Alabama. The painting was made at Washington, D. C.

Trumpet Creeper family. Bignoniaceae

Pl. 351. Trumpet Creeper
Campsis radicans

Trumpet Creeper is a vine which climbs on tree trunks, fences and cliffs, adhering by small roots sent out by the stem. The large leaves are compound, each divided into a number of leaflets arranged along the sides of a long midrib. There are 4 stamens in 2 sizes. The ovary becomes a long bean-like pod containing a number of flat seeds which bear thin wings.

Trumpet Creeper inhabits woods, roadsides and cliffs from New Jersey to Florida and westward to Iowa, Missouri and Texas. It is the state flower of Kentucky. The painting was made at Washington, D. C.

Pl. 352. Cross-vine
Anisostichus capreolatus

Cross-vine resembles Trumpet Creeper in its flowers, but differs in its leaves, which bear only 2 leaflets and a tendril at the end; the tendrils bear adhesive discs by means of which the plant climbs. The fruit also is like that of *Campsis,* but flat. The name is derived from the pith of the stem, which, when cut across, has the shape of a cross.

Cross-vine is found in swamps and along streams in woods on the coastal plain from Florida to Louisiana and northward to Maryland, southern Ohio and southern Missouri. The plant illustrated was collected near Beaufort, South Carolina.

Madder family. Rubiaceae

Pl. 353. Bedstraw *Galium boreale*

Bedstraw is a perennial which reaches a height of 3 feet and more. The square stem bears leaves in fours. In the tiny flowers the sepals are joined; the petals are joined to form a tube which is 3- or 4-lobed at the end; and the inferior ovary is 2-chambered. There are 3 or 4 stamens. The fruit is a small, 2-lobed bristly pod.

Bedstraw grows in open woods and thickets along streams from Nova Scotia and Quebec to Delaware and westward to Alaska, Colorado and New Mexico. The painting was made from a plant collected near Banff, Alberta.

Pl. 354. Bluets, Quaker Ladies
Houstonia caerulea

Houstonia flowers have their parts in fours except the pistil, which has 2 chambers in the ovary and 2 narrow stigmas on its style. The petals are joined in their basal parts into a short tube; their ends spread out as 4 lobes. The ovary is half-inferior; i.e., the receptacle or end of the stem rises around it and is joined to it about halfway up. This species grows from a slender creeping underground stem, and rises only about 6 inches from the ground.

Houstonia caerulea inhabits meadows from Nova Scotia and Quebec to Wisconsin and southward to Georgia and Arkansas; it is more common in the eastern parts of its range. The plant illustrated was collected near Washington, D. C.

Pl. 355. Partridge-berry *Mitchella repens*

The flowers of Partridge-berry grow in pairs, and the basal parts merge together in each pair forming a sort of double flower. The parts are all in fours. The flowers are of 2 forms, one having long stamens and a short style, the other a long style and short stamens.

Partridge-berry inhabits woods from Nova Scotia to Florida and westward in scattered places to Minnesota and Texas. The plant shown was found near Beaufort, South Carolina.

[57]

Honeysuckle family.
Caprifoliaceae

Pl. 356 Squashberry, Cranberry-bush
Viburnum pauciflorum

Viburnum is a large genus; most of the species are natives of eastern Asia; many are cultivated. They have 5 sepals, 5 joined petals, 5 stamens which protrude beyond the petals, and a 3-chambered inferior ovary. The style is very short or lacking, so that the three stigmas are situated at the summit of the ovary itself. Only one of the compartments of the ovary matures its seed; the two others abort. The fruit is like that of a cherry; the fleshy part encloses a stone in which is the single seed. The flowers of some species have a rather fetid odor.

Squashberry grows in moist woods from Labrador to Alaska and southward to Pennsylvania, Michigan, Minnesota, Colorado and Oregon. The branch shown was taken from a plant growing in the Columbia River Valley in British Columbia, at an altitude of 2,500 feet.

Pl. 357. Red-berried Elder
Sambucus pubens

This shrub grows to a height of 10 feet. The flowers are small, with 5 white petals joined together, from 3 to 5 stamens, and an inferior ovary with from 3 to 5 chambers; the style is 3-lobed at the tip. The leaves are pale and downy on the under side.

Red-berried Elder grows in rich woods from Newfoundland to Alaska and southward to Georgia, Indiana, Illinois, Colorado and British Columbia. The plant shown was found near Glacier, British Columbia, at an altitude of 3,500 feet.

Pl. 358, 359. Honeysuckle
Lonicera glaucescens

The Honeysuckles are shrubs or climbing vines. The united petals spread into 5 lobes which are often of unequal size; the lower side of the petal-tube may be expanded into a sort of sac. The flowers grow in pairs or threes and have no stalks of their own; sometimes they merge together. The 2- or 3-chambered inferior ovary becomes a berry. *Lonicera glaucescens* is a climbing shrub with leaves that are hairy on the under side. Under each group of yellow flowers is a pair of leaves joined so that they form a sort of disc, from the middle of which the flowers and fruit grow.

This Honeysuckle is found in woods and thickets from Ontario to Mackenzie and British Columbia and southward to Michigan, Iowa and Oklahoma. The plants illustrated came from Alberta: the flowering specimen from Lake Minnewonka near Banff, at at altitude of 4,500 feet; the fruiting branch from the Kootenay Valley near Lake Louise, at an altitude of 3,000 feet.

Pl. 360. Bearberry Honeysuckle
Lonicera involucrata

This is a shrub which grows up to 10 feet high. The yellow petals are all much alike in size and shape. The leaves underneath a pair of flowers become large, thick, and often bright red, as shown in the painting.

Bearberry Honeysuckle grows in moist woods and meadows from Quebec to British Columbia and southward to New Mexico and California. The plant shown was found near Hector, British Columbia, at an altitude of 4,000 feet.

Pl. 361. Trumpet Honeysuckle
Lonicera sempervirens

Trumpet Honeysuckle is a woody climber. Under each group of flowers there is one, and often two, pairs of leaves joined to form discs. The leaves are usually gray-green in color. It is named for the narrow flaring tubes formed by its petals, which are red outside and yellow inside; all the petals are alike in size and shape. The species is found in woods and thickets from Maine to Florida and westward to Nebraska and Texas; in the northern parts of this range it is not native but has escaped from cultivation; in the southern parts it is evergreen. The painting was made from a collection made in Yemassee, South Carolina.

Pl. 362. Twinflower *Linnaea borealis*

Linnaea was named after Linnaeus, often called the father of botany, because he gave us the first usable classification of plants and the system of naming plants which we still use; this species was a favorite with him. It has a slender creeping stem from which the flowering branches arise; they may stand up to 8 inches high. The petals are all alike. There are 4 stamens, 2 shorter than the others. The ovary is 3-chambered, but forms a 1-seeded fruit. The flowers are fragrant.

Linnaea borealis grows around the world in the northern regions. The American variety differs somewhat from the European and Asiatic plants; it is found in woods and on peaty slopes from Greenland and Labrador to Alaska and southward to Maryland, West Virginia, Ohio, South Dakota, Colorado, Utah and California. The plant illustrated was gathered near Lake Louise, Alberta, at an altitude of 5,500 feet.

Valerian family.
Valerianaceae

Pl. 363. Valerian *Valeriana sitchensis*

This Valerian stands about 2 feet tall. The flowers are small, each having 5 nearly equal joined petals (the tube is somewhat enlarged on one side), 3 stamens, and an ovary which has some indications of 3 compartments, but only one of these has an ovule and develops into the fruit. The sepals are replaced by feathery bristles, at first rolled inward, which spread out as the fruit develops.

Valeriana sitchensis grows in moist places at high altitudes from Alaska to Oregon and eastward to Idaho. The plant shown was found near Hector, British Columbia, at an altitude of 5,000 feet.

Bluebell family. Campanulaceae

Pl. 364. Alpine Harebell
Campanula lasiocarpa
The Alpine Harebell grows only 6 inches high or less. Its flowers are regular and their parts mostly in fives; the stigma, however, has 4 parts and the ovary 4 chambers. It grows in arctic and alpine regions from Alaska to British Columbia and Alberta; also in northeastern Asia. The plant in the painting was gathered on Eagle Peak near Glacier, British Columbia, at an altitude of 8,000 feet.

Pl. 365. Harebell, Bluebell
Campanula rotundifolia
Rotundifolia means "round-leaved"; but this applies only to the leaves at the base of the stem, which have rounded blades on long stalks; they soon wither and disappear, and the leaves usually found with the flowers are like those in the painting. The stem rises as much as 18 inches above the ground. The petals vary in color from white to blue. There are 3 branches at the summit of the style.

Campanula rotundifolia is the Bluebell of Scotland, and grows on rock ledges and banks and in meadows in all the northern parts of the world. It is highly variable, and the western American plants are often classified in a separate species, *Campanula petiolata;* however, the variation in the population and the importance to be attached to the different characters are not well understood. In America this species is found from Labrador to Alaska and southward to New Jersey, Pennsylvania, Ohio, Illinois, Missouri, Nebraska, Texas, Nuevo León, New Mexico, Arizona, and California. The painting was made from a plant collected near Hector, British Columbia, at an altitude of 4,000 feet.

Pl. 366. Brook Lobelia *Lobelia kalmii*
Lobelia is distinguished from *Campanula* by the fact that the petals are not joined all the way around; the tube which they make is split along the upper side. At the end their tips form 2 lips, with 2 usually sharp lobes above and 3 below. There are 5 stamens, the heads of which are joined around the style. The inferior ovary has 2 compartments. *Lobelia kalmii* grows up to about 2 feet tall.

It is found on wet rocks and shores and in swamps from Newfoundland to Mackenzie and southward to New Jersey, Pennsylvania, Ohio, Indiana, Illinois, Iowa, South Dakota, Colorado and British Columbia. The plant illustrated came from Canal Flats, British Columbia, at an altitude of 3,000 feet.

Pl. 367. Cardinal Flower *Lobelia cardinalis*
Cardinal Flower may grow to a height of nearly 6 feet. Its tube of petals is not only split along the upper side but has openings along the other sides as well. The brilliant color is distinctive.

Cardinal Flower grows by streams and in wet places from New Brunswick to Minnesota and southward to Florida and Texas. The painting was made at Pocono Manor, Pennsylvania.

Composite family. Compositae

The Composite Family is the largest of all our families of plants, with some 15,000 species; it includes many familiar weeds (Ragweed, Tickseed, Yarrow, Oxeye Daisy, Dandelion, Thistle, Cocklebur, Burdock) besides cultivated plants (Dahlia, Chrysanthemum, Zinnia, Marigold, Aster, Lettuce). Its chief peculiarity is that the flowers are small and are closely grouped into a head which most persons think of as a single flower. The flowers of one head may be all alike, as they are in the Dandelion; or there may be a ring of ray flowers surrounding a central group of disc flowers, as in the Sunflower. The individual flower has an inferior ovary above which rises the tube formed by the 5 joined petals — which may spread at one side into a ray if it is a ray flower, or if all the flowers are alike and raylike. There are no proper sepals, but just outside the petals, where we should expect sepals, is often a pappus, a ring of scales or bristles or sometimes just a ridge. The fruit is what we usually think of as the seed (e.g., of a Sunflower or Dandelion); that is, it is the stem-end surrounding the matured ovary inside which is a single seed. The pappus often remains attached to this fruit, as with the Dandelion. The disc on which the flowers grow may also bear scales called chaff; and around the entire group of flowers is one or several rings of more or less leaf-like bracts, forming the involucre.

Pl. 368. Black-eyed Susan *Rudbeckia hirta*
Black-eyed Susan grows up to 3 feet tall and even more. It is usually hairy, with stiff harsh hairs all over. The yellow rays lack pistil and stamens — they are neutral; the dark-colored disc flowers form the fruit and seeds. The disc is convex and bears chaff; the pappus consists of a short crown.

Rudbeckia hirta grows in fields and waste land from Nova Scotia to Florida and westward to Manitoba, Colorado and Texas.

Pl. 369. Sunflower *Helianthus strumosus*
The many species of *Helianthus* are rather difficult to distinguish. They all have neutral ray flowers and

fertile disc flowers; the disc is flat and bears chaff mixed with the flowers; the pappus consists of two scales which taper to a bristle-like point. *Helianthus strumosus* may reach a height of 6 feet. It is perennial, with rough leaves; each harsh hair rises from a tubercle-like base which can be seen with a magnifier. The bracts are smooth except at the edges, where they are fringed with minute hairs.

Helianthus strumosus grows in woodlands from Maine and Ontario to Florida and westward to North Dakota and Texas. A species of *Helianthus* is the state flower of Kansas, where several species of the genus abound.

Pl. 370. Balsam-root
Balsamorhiza sagittata

The thick root, which is perennial, is aromatic, and in former days was used as food by the Indians. The stem grows to a height of 2 feet; both it and the leaves are silvery with fine matted hairs. Most of the leaves grow on long stalks at the base of the stem. Both ray and disc flowers form achenes; the projecting branched styles are well shown in the painting, as is the way in which the disc flowers open in order from the outside toward the center. The disc is flat or slightly convex. There is no pappus.

This species of Balsam-root grows on dry hillsides from South Dakota to British Columbia and southward to Colorado and California. The plant illustrated was collected near Radium Hot Springs, British Columbia, at an altitude of 3,500 feet.

Pl. 371. Golden Star
Chrysogonum virginianum

This plant rarely reaches a height of 2 feet. The rays are pistillate and fertile, and the disc flowers furnish only pollen. The disc is flat and chaffy. The pappus is a cup-shaped crown. The fruits are enclosed by the bracts, which fall with them.

Chrysogonum is found in woodlands from Pennsylvania to Florida and Alabama. The painting was made at Washington, D. C.

Pl. 372. Perennial Gaillardia
Gaillardia aristata

Gaillardia may grow to a height of more than 2 feet. The rays, which are cleft in 3 at the end, are neutral and bear no fruit. The disc flowers vary from red or purple to brownish-yellow. The disc is convex and bears bristle-like chaff. The pappus consists of 6 to 10 long-pointed scales.

Gaillardia aristata grows in meadows and prairies from Saskatchewan to British Columbia and southward• to New Mexico and Arizona. The specimen shown was gathered at Emerald Lake near Field, British Columbia, at an altitude of 6,000 feet.

Pl. 373. Yarrow *Achillea lanulosa*

Yarrow is a perennial herb growing from a creeping underground stem; it may rise to a height of 2 feet. This species is closely related to the common weed of the same name, but is more woolly; both are strongly aromatic. The rays, which are occasionally pink, are pistillate. The disc is convex, chaffy. There is no pappus.

This Yarrow occurs on gravelly or sandy shores and in open ground from Newfoundland to British Columbia and southward to New England, Michigan, Missouri, and into Mexico. The painting was made from a plant found on the Red Deer River north of Lake Louise, Alberta, at an altitude of 6,700 feet.

ASTER, FLEABANE AND GOLDENROD
ASTER, ERIGERON, SOLIDAGO

These three genera are similar, and each contains a large number of species which are very difficult to distinguish. All have a disc which is flat and lacks chaff. The pappus of all consists of fine bristles, usually white in color. The ray flowers of all are pistillate and form fruit. *Aster* has an involucre composed of 2 or more rows of overlapping bracts; *Solidago* is similar in this respect. *Erigeron* has usually only one row of bracts which scarcely overlap. In *Aster* the ray flowers vary from white to blue, purple or lavender, or occasionally pink. In *Erigeron* much the same range of color is found. *Solidago* is distinguished by its yellow ray flowers.

Pl. 374. New England Aster
Aster novae-angliae

New England Aster is characterized by leaves which are auriculate at the base; that is, each has two "ears" projecting around the stem. The whole plant is hairy and somewhat sticky, and the leaves are harsh to the touch. There are 45 to 100 ray flowers, often colored a deep violet or purple, occasionally white or pink. *Aster novae-angliae* grows in meadows and woodland openings from Quebec to Maryland and westward to Alberta, Kansas and Kentucky.

Pl. 375. Pineland Aster *Aster walteri*

This Aster has basal leaves which are broader near the tip than farther down. The leaves on the stem are rigid and reflexed; they become very small as one approaches the flowerheads. The species grows in pinelands on the coastal plain from North Carolina to Florida.

Pl. 376. Prairie Aster *Aster campestris*

The Prairie Aster grows only to a height of 18 inches. It is smooth or nearly so, and has narrow leaves which have no stalks. It grows in valleys from Colorado to Oregon and British Columbia. The plant illustrated was collected near Radium Hot Springs, British Columbia, at an altitude of 3,000 feet.

Pl. 377. Fleabane *Erigeron peregrinus*

Erigeron peregrinus has been divided into several subspecies and varieties. At one time it was considered a species of *Aster,* which is evidence of the artificial nature of the distinction between these genera. The plant is smooth or nearly so, the leaves lance-shaped, or those at the base of the stem broader towards the tip. The bracts are very narrow and reddish, and spread loosely, as is shown in the painting. The long rays are red at first, and become violet or purple as they mature. The species grows in moist places high in the mountains from Alaska to California and eastward to Colorado and New Mexico. The painting was made at Lake Louise, from a plant gathered at an altitude of 7,500 feet.

Pl. 378.   Meadow Fleabane
Erigeron speciosus

This species reaches a height of nearly 3 feet. It is smooth or nearly so, except for the fringe of small hairs usually present along the edges of the leaves. The leaves vary from lance-shaped to broader towards the tip, and the basal leaves are not much larger than those on the stem. It grows on mountains from South Dakota to British Columbia and southward to New Mexico, Arizona and Oregon. The plant shown was gathered on the Ghost River near Banff, Alberta, at an altitude of 4,000 feet.

Pl. 379.   Fleabane   *Erigeron caespitosus*

This Fleabane is whitish with small hairs that grow all over it. The stem grows only to about a foot high. The basal leaves are broadest near the tip. The rays vary in color from white or blue to pink. The species is found in dry, often rocky, places from Alaska to Washington and eastward and southward to Saskatchewan, North Dakota, Nebraska, Utah and New Mexico. The plant illustrated was collected in the Saskatchewan River Valley in Alberta, at an altitude of 3,500 feet.

Pl. 380.   Golden Fleabane   *Erigeron aureus*

Yellow is a rather rare color in the ray flowers of *Erigeron*. This small species grows only about 6 inches high. Its leaves are finely hairy. It grows in rocky places mostly above timberline from Alberta to British Columbia and Washington. The plant shown was found on the summit of Mt. Fairview, near Lake Louise, Alberta, at an altitude of 8,500 feet.

Pl. 381.   Aleutian Fleabane
Erigeron humilis

This plant grows about 10 inches tall. It is more or less hairy, although it often becomes smooth as it matures. The rays vary in color from white to purplish. The bracts of the involucre are woolly and blackish or purple. *Erigeron humilis* grows in northern regions around the world; in America it extends southward to Labrador, Quebec, Montana, Alberta and British Columbia. The painting was made from a plant gathered in the Little Yoho Valley near Field, British Columbia, at an altitude of 7,500 feet.

Pl. 382.   Goldenrod   *Solidago canadensis*

This common species of Goldenrod has leaves which decrease gradually in size from the base of the plant upward, rather than having large basal leaves and small leaves on the stem as some other species have. The sharp-toothed leaves usually have 3 main ribs extending from the base; they have no stalks. The heads of flowers are rather small, only 1/8 inch or less high; they are crowded along the upper side of many curving branches which form a pyramidal flower cluster. The species is highly variable; some plants are almost smooth, while others have harsh gray hairs and still others loose soft hairs.

Solidago canadensis is found in open places from Newfoundland to Saskatchewan and southward to North Carolina, Tennessee and New Mexico.

Pl. 383.   Sidesaddle Goldenrod
Solidago ciliosa

This is a small species; the stems are likely to lean on the ground and rise only about 8 inches above it. The plant is hairy. The leaves may be toothed towards the tip, and are fringed with short hairs. The rays are rather long for a Goldenrod. *Solidago ciliosa* grows at high altitudes from Colorado to Arizona and westward to British Columbia. The plant illustrated was collected near Field, British Columbia, at an altitude of 6,500 feet.

Pl. 384.   Pearly Everlasting
Anaphalis margaritacea

Pearly Everlasting has two sorts of plants which may be called male and female. The former has staminate flowers only, the latter mainly pistillate flowers (often with a few staminate flowers in the center of each head). The flowers are all tubular; there are no rays. The disc is flat and there is no chaff. The pappus consists of fine bristles. The bracts of the involucre are dry and pearly-white, remaining attached for a long time. The plant is covered with a dense white wool.

Pearly Everlasting grows in dry open places, often in sandy soil, from Newfoundland to Alaska and southward to North Carolina, Ohio, Wisconsin, New Mexico and California. The plant shown in the painting was collected on Moose Creek in the Kootenay Valley, Alberta, at an altitude of 3,500 feet.

Pl. 385.   Pink Everlasting
Antennaria rosea

Antennaria resembles *Anaphalis* in many ways. The bristles of the pappus, however, are often thickened toward the end, and those of the pistillate flowers are joined at the base so that they fall all together. Staminate flowers are rare or even unknown in many species; their fruits and seeds mature without fertilization. Pink Everlasting grows 18 inches tall. Like most of the species of this genus it is covered with white wool. The bracts are pink or red.

Antennaria rosea is found in mountain meadows from South Dakota to Yukon and southward to Colorado and California. The specimen illustrated came from Lake Agnes, Alberta, at an altitude of 6,000 feet.

[61]

Pl. 386.   Howell's Everlasting
                          Antennaria howellii

Like many species of *Antennaria,* this one forms
leafy creeping stems, from which the flowering stems
arise in the following year; they may grow a foot high.
The bracts are tinged with brown or red. The painting shows the fruiting condition. *Antennaria howellii*
grows in woods from Montana to British Columbia
and southward to Oregon. The plant shown was collected on the Siffleur River in Alberta, at an altitude
of 5,000 feet.

Various species of *Antennaria* are known as Pussy-
toes or Ladies' Tobacco.

Pl. 387.   Brown Everlasting
                          Antennaria luzuloides

This rather large species sends its stems up 2 feet
or more from a woody stem underground; the involucre is ¼ inch high. It grows in dry areas with
grass and sagebrush from Wyoming to British Columbia and southward into California. This specimen also was collected on the Siffleur River, at an
altitude of 4,500 feet.

Pl. 388.   Woolly Arnica   *Arnica tomentosa*

The heads of *Arnica* usually have ray flowers which
are yellow and pistillate. The disc is flat and without
chaff and may be hairy. The pappus is composed of a
few bristles which may be white or brownish and are
rather rigid and rough. The medicinal preparation
known as arnica is made from the dried flowers of
certain species, and is used in the treatment of bruises
and sprains.

Arnica tomentosa derives both its Latin and English names from the white wool which covers the entire plant. It grows up to a foot high, and is found in
gravelly soil mainly in the mountains from Montana
to British Columbia and Alaska; also in Newfoundland. The specimen painted was found on the Siffleur River in Alberta, at an altitude of 5,000 feet.

Pl. 389.   Lake Louise Arnica
                          Arnica louiseana

This is another mountain species which grows usually only about 8 inches high from the creeping underground stem. The stem is woolly but the leaves usually become smooth as they mature. It grows on alpine slopes and meadows in the Rocky Mountains of
Alberta, and also in rocky places in Newfoundland
and the Gaspé Peninsula. The plant illustrated was
gathered on the headwaters of the Clearwater River
in Alberta.

GROUNDSEL, RAGWORT, BUTTERWEED
SENECIO

Senecio is an enormous genus, containing over
1,000 species; many of those in South America are
shrubs or trees. Over 100 species have been found in
our western states. The genus is characterized by a

[62]

pappus composed of numerous soft white bristles
(which give it its name, derived from the Latin meaning "old man"). The disc is flat, without chaff. The
bracts are usually in one row, with sometimes some of
a smaller size at the base. Ray flowers are lacking in
many species; when present, they are pistillate. Many
species are hard to distinguish; some hybridize freely.

Pl. 390.   Mourning Ragwort
                          Senecio lugens

Senecio lugens reaches a height of about a foot. It
is smooth and grayish-green, with toothed leaves. The
rays are long and narrow. It grows in wet places from
Alaska southward and eastward to Idaho. The specimen shown was found on the Pipestone River near
Lake Louise, Alberta, at an altitude of 5,000 feet. The
curious Latin name — of which the English is simply a translation — was given in commemoration of
an Indian massacre.

Pl. 391.   Few-flowered Groundsel
                          Senecio pauciflorus

This plant is smooth and grows to a height of 2
feet. The leaves are rather thick; those at the base of
the stem have long stalks, the blade being more or less
heart-shaped and coarsely toothed. Ray flowers are
lacking; the disc flowers vary from orange to reddish.
The species occurs in meadows and on alpine slopes
from Labrador and the Gaspé Peninsula to Alaska
and southward to Wyoming and California. The
plant illustrated was found on Johnson Creek near
Lake Louise, at an altitude of 5,500 feet.

Pl. 392.   Arrow-leaf Ragwort
                          Senecio triangularis

Arrow-leaf Ragwort grows to a height of nearly 6
feet. It is smooth when mature. The leaves vary
greatly in shape, some of them being arrow-shaped
with teeth or notches along the sides, on long stalks.
The species is found along streams at various altitudes
from Colorado to British Columbia and Alaska and
southward to New Mexico and California. The painting was made from a plant collected near Evelyn Glacier in Alberta, at an altitude of 6,500 feet.

Pl. 393.   Butterbur   *Petasites hyperboreus*

Butterbur has two sorts of heads which appear on
different plants. One sort contains flowers (both ray
and disc) which apparently have both stamens and
pistils, but furnish only pollen and make no fruit;
the other head is composed of pistillate flowers which
form fruit. *Petasites hyperboreus* has fragrant purplish
flowers; the stem is woolly and about a foot high,
growing from a thick creeping stem. The leaves are
triangular, on long stalks, white and woolly on the
under side. The painting shows a fruiting specimen,
in which the pappus of soft white bristles is evident.

Petasites hyperboreus grows from Hudson Bay to
Alaska and southward to Alberta and Washington.
The plant shown was found in Vermilion Pass, Al-
berta, at an altitude of 6,500 feet.

Pl. 394. Joe-Pye Weed
Eupatorium purpureum

Joe-Pye Weed may grow to a height of 6 feet, a coarse strong plant with sharply toothed leaves in groups of from 2 to 5. The stem is purple at the joints. There are numerous heads clustered in a broad inflorescence at the summit of the plant; each head contains only about half a dozen flowers, all tubular, with no rays. The petals vary greatly in color, from whitish to pale pink or lilac. The pappus is composed of bristles. The plant has the scent of vanilla when it is crushed or bruised.

Joe-Pye Weed grows in woods from New England to Florida and westward to Minnesota and Oklahoma.

Pl. 395. White Thistle
Cirsium hookerianum

The genus *Cirsium* includes the common thistles, with usually spiny stems, leaves bearing spines at the ends of their teeth, and spiny tips to the bracts. The disc is flattish and bears numerous bristles instead of chaff. The flowers are all tubular — there are no rays. The pappus is formed of feathery bristles, each bristle bearing many fine branches; they are spoken of as plumose. The bristles of one flower are joined at the base and fall all together. *Cirsium hookerianum* grows to a height of 2 feet. Its leaves are densely woolly on the lower side, and the bracts bear long tangled white hairs.

The White Thistle grows in the mountains from Montana to British Columbia. The specimen illustrated was found in Vermilion Pass, Alberta, at an altitude of 5,400 feet.

Pl. 396. Wavy-leaved or Prairie Thistle
Cirsium undulatum

Cirsium undulatum is a stout species which may grow 4 feet tall. The inner bracts have thin dry tips without spines. The leaves are covered with fine white wool on the under side, and the upper side also is usually woolly. This Thistle is found in prairies and other dry open places from Michigan to British Columbia and southward to Missouri, Texas, New Mexico, Arizona and California. The painting was made at Radium Hot Springs, British Columbia, 3,500 feet above the sea.

Pl. 397. Saussurea   *Saussurea densa*

Saussurea resembles *Cirsium* except in lacking spines. The plumose pappus-bristles are surrounded by a second circle of shorter bristles. This species grows to a height of only about 8 inches, its leaves crowded. The leaves and the bracts are covered with tangled white hairs like a spider's web. The purple flowers are all tubular. The disc is flat and chaffy.

Saussurea densa grows in the higher mountains of the Canadian Rockies and is rather rare. The plant illustrated was collected near Lake Louise, at an altitude of 7,000 feet.

AGOSERIS, GOAT CHICORY
AGOSERIS

Pl. 398. Slender Agoseris   *Agoseris gracilens*

The genus *Agoseris* resembles the common Dandelion in appearance. The leaves are all basal from a thick tap-root, and the stem bears a single head of flowers. The flowers are all ray-like or strap-shaped. The disc has no chaff. The pappus is composed of white bristles.

This species has orange or reddish petals. The leaves are very variable both in shape and in their covering of wool. The flower-stalk stands about a foot high. The painting shows the fruiting stage, with the spreading white pappus forming a crown on each fruit.

Slender Agoseris grows in moist ground from Wyoming to British Columbia and southward to Colorado and California. The plant shown was found near Douglas Lake, Alberta, at an altitude of 7,000 feet.

Pl. 399. Grass-leaved Agoseris
Agoseris graminifolia

This species is smooth or nearly so, and more or less glaucous (i.e., gray-green with a waxy coating). The flowering stem grows a foot high. The orange flowers turn purple when they are dried. It grows in meadows from Alberta and British Columbia to Utah and Arizona. The painting was made at Lake Louise, Alberta; the plant grew at an altitude of 5,700 feet.

Pl. 400. Woolly Agoseris   *Agoseris villosa*

Villosa means woolly and sufficiently indicates the character of this species. The flowering stem grows about a foot high. The painting shows the stout perennial taproot from which leaves and stem grow. The light yellow flowers turn pinkish with age. The species grows in the mountains from Montana to British Columbia and southward into Utah. The plant shown was collected near Glacier Lake, Alberta, at an altitude of 7,500 feet.

This chart provides a convenient means for identifying the wild flowers shown in this book. There are, however, thousands of other species which grow wild in North America. If a plant can be fitted into one of the classes shown in the chart, it may probably be referred to one of the corresponding families or genera, or to one of their relatives. In this way the search for the precise species is narrowed down considerably.

For the technical terms used in the chart, the reader is referred to the Glossary on page 9.

I. The cone-bearing plants, all woody, with narrow leaves which are often needle-like and which mostly remain on the plant through the winter (the exception is *Larix*, PL. 5).

Pine and Cypress Families, PL. 1-11.

II. The flowering plants, woody and herbaceous, with leaves of various shapes but rarely needle-like and mostly falling in the autumn. See A-O below.

A. Plants lacking green color.
Monotropa, PL. 278.
Hypopitys, PL. 279, 280.
Orobanche, PL. 349.
Conopholis, PL. 350.

B. Plants growing attached to other plants and lacking contact with the ground (parasites and epiphytes).
Tillandsia, PL. 22.
Epidendrum, PL. 89, 90.
Cyrtopodium, PL. 91.
Phoradendron, PL. 98.

C. Plants growing in water (the flowers emerging).
Sagittaria, PL. 12.
Pontederia, PL. 21.
Water-lily Family, PL. 106, 107.
Menyanthes, PL. 305.

D. Prickly cushion-like cacti.
Cactus Family, PL. 233-235.

E. Orchids, with the lower petal (the lip) usually large and differently shaped and/or colored from the others, and the stamen(s) united with the style and stigma.
Orchid Family, PL. 67-91.

F. Herbaceous plants with leaves shaped like pitchers or vases, in which insects are trapped.
Pitcher-plant Family, PL. 151-158.

G. Herbaceous plants with small flowers crowded in a thick spike which is generally enveloped by a single large leaf; the latter is often colored and may be mistaken for a petal.
Arum Family, PL. 15-19.

H. Grass-like plants with small flowers lacking obvious perianth and crowded together in scaly clusters.
Sedge Family, PL. 13, 14.

I. Herbaceous plants with small flowers gathered in heads which simulate flowers; in one head the actual flowers are tubular or strap-shaped or both (the latter then forming rays around a central disc).
Composite Family, PL. 368-400.

J. Shrubs or small trees, without colored perianth, their flowers in catkins.
Salix and *Alnus*, PL. 92-96.

K. Herbaceous and woody plants with papilionaceous flowers and leaves mostly divided into leaflets.
part of Bean Family, PL. 192-206.

L. Vines, climbing by tendrils attached to other plants or to fences, etc., or by twining around them.
Clematis, PL. 128-131.
Wisteria, PL. 203.
Vicia, PL. 205.
Lathyrus, PL. 206.
Passiflora, PL. 232.
Gelsemium, PL. 295.
Campsis, PL. 351.
Anisostichus, PL. 352.
Lonicera, PL. 358-361.

M. Woody plants (trees and shrubs), with flowers of various types, other than those in J-L. See 1-23 below.

	LEAVES	PERIANTH	STAMENS	PISTIL(S)	
1.	attached singly, often large.	large white or greenish sepals.	many.	many.	Magnolia Family, PL. 132-137.
2.	attached singly.	3 green sepals, 6 brown-purple petals.	many.	several.	*Asimina*, PL. 138.
3.	attached singly, usually with stipules; often divided.	about 5 sepals, 5 petals.	many.	one or more in a head or in a cup-shaped receptacle.	part of Rose Family, PL. 168, 170, 179-185.
4.	attached singly.	about 5 sepals, 5 petals.	many.	one, with inferior ovary.	Apple Family, PL. 186-190.
5.	attached singly.	4 sepals, 5 petals.	many.	one.	Tea Family, PL. 224, 225.
6.	attached singly.	5 sepals, often minute, 5 petals.	5.	one, with inferior ovary.	*Ribes*, PL. 165, 166. *Oplopanax*, PL. 245.
7.	attached singly.	4 sepals, 4 strap-shaped narrow petals.	8.	one, with 2 styles.	*Hamamelis*, PL. 167.
8.	attached in pairs.	4 small colored sepals, no petals.	8.	one.	*Shepherdia*, PL. 236.
9.	attached singly, each pinnately divided.	6 sepals, 6 petals, several bracts, all small, yellow.	6.	one, becoming a blue berry.	*Mahonia*, PL. 139.
10.	attached singly.	4-6 sepals, 4-8 petals, all small.	as many as petals.	one, becoming a red or black berry.	*Ilex*, PL. 212-214.
11.	attached singly, often lobed.	5 sepals, 5 large petals, several bracts.	many, all joined in a column around the style.	one, with 5-branched style.	*Hibiscus*, PL. 221.
12.	attached singly, silvery or evergreen.	4 or 5 yellow sepals, no petals.	as many as sepals.	one.	*Elaeagnus*, PL. 237, 238. *Fremontia*, PL. 223.
13.	attached singly, evergreen.	2 sepals, 4 yellow petals.	many.	one.	*Dendromecon*, PL. 143.
14.	attached singly, small.	5 sepals, often minute, 5 petals joined to form a hanging cup or urn.	8-10.	one, with inferior ovary, becoming a berry.	Blueberry Family, PL. 281-286.
15.	attached singly or sometimes in pairs or whorls, or basal or crowded.	4 or 5 sepals, 4 or 5 petals joined at the base.	5-10.	one.	Heath Family, PL. 251-272. Diapensia Family, PL. 287, 288.
16.	attached singly, needle-like.	3 sepals, no petals.	3.	one, becoming berry-like.	*Empetrum*, PL. 211.
17.	attached in pairs, palmately divided.	5 sepals, 4 or 5 unequal petals.	7.	one, becoming a tough round pod.	*Aesculus*, PL. 217.
18.	attached in pairs, palmately lobed.	5 sepals, 5 petals, all small.	3-6.	one, 2-lobed, becoming a winged "key."	*Acer*, PL. 215, 216.
19.	attached in pairs.	4 sepals, 4 petals joined at base; cluster of flowers sometimes surrounded by petal-like bracts.	4.	one, with inferior ovary, becoming a berry-like fruit.	part of Dogwood Family, PL. 246-248.
20.	attached in pairs.	4 sepals, 4 petals joined at base.	4.	one, becoming a purplish fruit.	*Callicarpa*, PL. 320

[65]

	LEAVES	PERIANTH	STAMENS	PISTIL(S)	
21.	attached in pairs.	5 small sepals, 5 petals joined at base.	5.	one, with inferior ovary, becoming a berry.	part of Honeysuckle Family, PL. 356-360.
22.	attached in pairs.	4 minute sepals, 4 strap-shaped petals joined at base.	2.	one, becoming an olive-like fruit.	Chionanthus, PL. 294.
23.	bunched above spines of stem.	5 sepals, 5 red petals, partly joined.	10 or more.	one, becoming a small pod.	Fouquieria, PL. 310.

N. Herbaceous plants other than those in A-I and K, and having separate petals or no petals (sometimes the sepals resemble petals). See 1-18 below.

	LEAVES	PERIANTH	STAMENS	PISTIL(S)	
1.	attached singly or in whorls, or basal.	6 parts, all alike or 3 green, 3 colored.	6.	one, becoming a berry or 3-chambered pod.	Lily Family, PL. 23-59. Tradescantia, PL. 20.
2.	chiefly basal, narrow or even grass-like.	6 parts, all more or less alike in color.	3 or 6.	one, with inferior ovary, becoming a 3-chambered pod.	Amaryllis and Iris Families, PL. 60-66.
3.	attached singly.	5 green sepals, no petals.	5.	one, with 1 or 2 styles.	Comandra, PL. 97. Chenopodium, PL. 100.
4.	basal, heart-shaped on stalks.	3 brown sepals, no petals.	12.	one, with inferior ovary.	Asarum, PL. 99.
5.	attached singly or basal, often palmately lobed or divided.	about 5 sepals, 5 petals or none; sometimes spurred.	many.	rarely one, usually several on a projecting receptacle.	part of Buttercup Family, PL. 108-127.
6.	attached singly.	4 sepals, 4 petals.	6, 4 longer than the other 2.	one, becoming a pod.	Mustard Family, PL. 148-150.
7.	attached singly or basal.	5 sepals, 5 petals.	5 or 10.	one, becoming a 1- to 5-chambered pod.	part of Saxifrage Family, PL. 160-164. Cassia, PL. 191. Geranium, PL. 207, 208.
8.	attached singly or basal, often lobed or divided, with stipules.	5 sepals, 5 petals.	many.	several or many, in a cup-shaped or on a projecting receptacle.	part of Rose Family, PL. 169, 171-178.
9.	attached singly, with stipules.	5 sepals, 5 petals, often 3 bracts.	many, joined in a column around the style.	one, with about 5 branches of the style.	part of Mallow Family, PL. 219, 220.
10.	attached singly or basal.	5 sepals, 5 petals, the lowest spurred.	5, cohering around the style.	one, becoming a pod with many seeds in one chamber.	Violet Family, PL. 226-231.
11.	attached in pairs.	5 sepals, 5 petals.	10.	one, with 3-5 styles.	Pink Family, PL. 101-103.
12.	attached in pairs.	2 sepals, 5 petals.	5.	one, with 3 styles or a 3-branched style.	Purslane Family, PL. 104, 105.
13.	one pair or basal.	4-6 sepals, 6-9 petals.	8 or more.	one.	part of Barberry Family, PL. 140, 141.
14.	attached singly or basal.	2 sepals, soon falling, 4-12 petals.	many.	one, becoming a pod.	Poppy Family, PL. 142-144.
15.	attached singly.	3 sepals, the lower yellow, much inflated and spurred; 3 petals.	5.	one, becoming a pod which opens explosively.	Impatiens, PL. 218.
16.	attached in pairs.	5 sepals, 5 yellow petals.	many, often in several bunches.	one, with several styles.	Hypericum, PL. 222.

[66]

	LEAVES	PERIANTH	STAMENS	PISTIL(S)	
17.	basal, folding along the midrib, the toothed edges interlocking, to trap insects.	5 sepals, 5 petals.	10-20, joined at base.	one.	*Dionaea,* PL. 159.
18.	basal, long-stalked.	3 sepals, 3 petals.	many, in separate flowers from pistils.	many, in separate flowers from stamens.	*Sagittaria,* PL. 12.

O. Herbaceous plants other than those in A-I, K and N, having petals united at least at their bases (if one petal is pulled off carefully, all of them come off together) or at their tips. See 1-14 below.

1.	attached singly or basal, delicately cut.	2 sepals, soon falling, 4 petals joined at tips, 1 or 2 spurred.	6, joined in 2 bunches.	one, becoming a pod.	Fumitory Family, PL. 145-147.
2.	attached singly, narrow.	5 sepals, 2 bearing wings, 3 petals, 1 crested.	6 or 8, joined in 2 sets.	one.	*Polygala,* PL. 209, 210.
3.	attached singly or in pairs or whorls.	4 sepals, 4 petals.	4 or 8.	one, with inferior ovary, becoming a narrow pod or a berry-like fruit.	Evening Primrose Family, PL. 239-244. part of Dogwood Family, PL. 249, 250. Madder Family, PL. 353-355.
4.	chiefly basal.	5 sepals, 5 petals, joined at base.	10.	one.	part of Wintergreen Family, PL. 273-277.
5.	basal.	5 sepals, 5 petals, their tips spreading or reflexed.	5, attached to the petals.	one.	Primrose Family, PL. 289-293.
6.	attached in pairs.	5 sepals, 5 petals, often pleated, all twisted together in bud.	5.	one, becoming a pod with many seeds in one chamber.	part of Gentian Family, PL. 296-304.
7.	attached in pairs.	5 sepals, 5 petals, all reflexed, with a crown.	5, attached to the stigma.	one, becoming a pod; the seeds bearing silky hairs.	*Asclepias,* PL. 306, 307.
8.	attached in pairs.	5 sepals, 5 petals forming a tube with flaring lobes.	5, attached to the petals.	one, three-chambered.	Phlox Family, PL. 308, 309.
9.	attached singly.	5 sepals, 5 petals, joined near base.	5, attached to the petals.	one, 2- or 4-chambered.	Waterleaf and Borage Families, PL. 311-318.
10.	attached in pairs.	5 sepals, 5 petals forming 2 lips.	2, or 4 in 2 pairs of unequal length.	one, 4-lobed.	part of Verbena Family, PL. 319; Mint Family, PL. 321-323.
11.	attached singly, in pairs or whorls, or basal.	5 sepals, 5 petals forming 2 lips.	2 or 4, attached to the petals (a rudimentary fifth stamen sometimes present).	one, 2-chambered.	Figwort Family, PL. 324-346. *Pinguicula,* PL. 347, 348.
12.	attached in pairs.	5 sepals, 5 petals nearly alike.	3 or 4.	one, with inferior ovary.	*Linnaea,* PL. 362. *Valeriana,* PL. 363.
13.	attached singly or basal.	5 sepals, 5 petals forming a bell.	5.	one, with inferior ovary.	*Campanula,* PL. 364, 365.
14.	attached singly.	5 sepals, 5 petals forming a tube split on the upper side and ending in 2 upper and 3 lower teeth.	5.	one, with inferior ovary.	*Lobelia,* PL. 366, 367.

Index

Plates 1-400

PLATE I   *Alpine Fir - Abies lasiocarpa*   MVW

PLATE 2   Engelmann Spruce - Picea engelmanni   MVW

PLATE 3   Mountain Hemlock - Tsuga mertensiana   MVW

PLATE 4   Douglas Fir – Pseudotsuga taxifolia   MVW

PLATE 5   *Western Larch - Larix occidentalis*   MVW

PLATE 6   *Limber Pine - Pinus flexilis*   MVW

PLATE 7   Long-leaved Pine - Pinus palustris   MVW

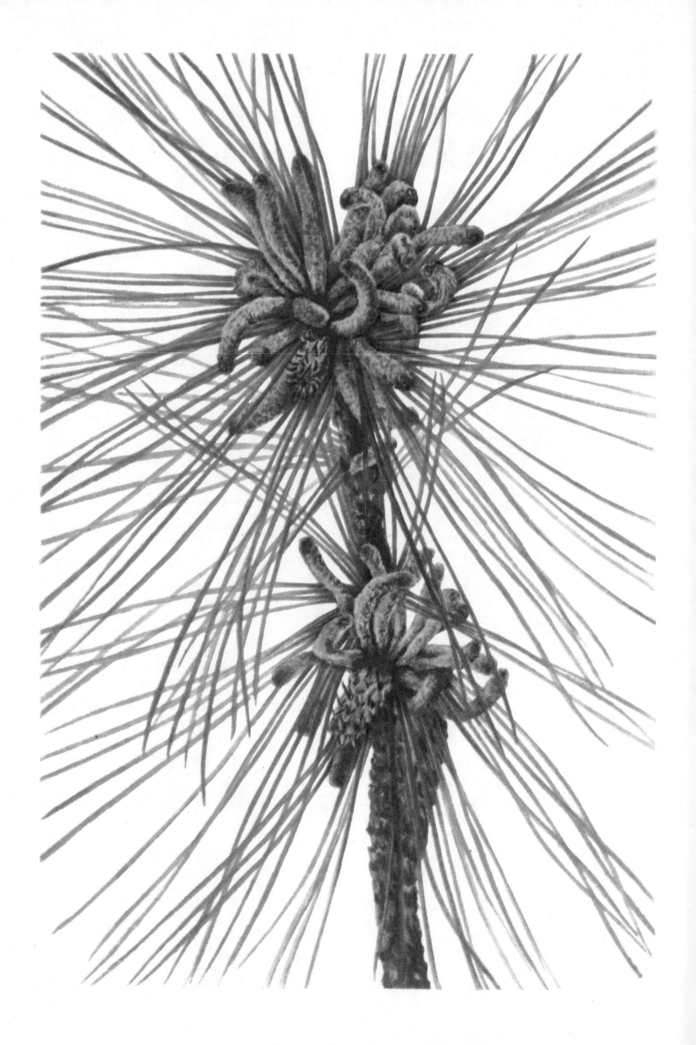

PLATE 8   *Loblolly Pine - Pinus taeda*   MVW

PLATE 9   *Western Red Cedar - Thuja plicata*   MVW

PLATE 10   *Creeping Juniper - Juniperus horizontalis*   MVW

PLATE II   *Mountain Juniper - Juniperus sibirica*   MVW

PLATE 12   Arrowleaf - Sagittaria cuneata   MVW

PLATE 13   Cotton Grass - Eriophorum chamissonis   MVW

PLATE 14   Golden Sedge - Carex aurea   MVW

PLATE 16   Green Dragon - Arisaema dracontium   MVW

PLATE 17   Wild Calla - Calla palustris   MVW

PLATE 18   Skunk Cabbage - Symplocarpus foetidus   MVW

PLATE 19   Golden Club - Orontium aquaticum   MVW

PLATE 20   Spiderwort - Tradescantia virginiana   MVW

PLATE 21   Pickerel Weed - Pontederia cordata   MVW

PLATE 22   *Tillandsia - Tillandsia fasciculata*   MVW

PLATE 23   *Bear-grass – Xerophyllum tenax*   MVW

PLATE 24   Glaucous Yygadene - Zygadenus elegans   MVW

PLATE 25 False Hellebore - Veratrum viride MVW

PLATE 26   *Fly-poison - Amianthium muscaetoxicum*   MVW

PLATE 27   Camass - Camassia quamash   MVW

PLATE 28   White Adder's-tongue, Dog-tooth Violet - Erythronium albidum   MVW

PLATE 29   Yellow Adder's-tongue, Dog-tooth Violet - Erythronium americanum   MVW

PLATE 30   Avalanche Lily - Erythronium montanum   MVW

PLATE 31   *Glacier Lily - Erythronium grandiflorum*   MVW

PLATE 32   Canada Lily - *Lilium canadense*   MVW

PLATE 33   *Turk's-cap Lily - Lilium superbum*   MVW

PLATE 34   *Columbia Lily - Lilium columbianum*   MVW

PLATE 35 Western Red Lily - Lilium umbellatum MVW

PLATE 36   *Catalina Mariposa - Calochortus catalinae*   MVW

PLATE 37 *Lilac Mariposa - Calochortus splendens* MVW

PLATE 38   Cat's Ear - Calochortus elegans   MVW

PLATE 39   Green-banded Mariposa, Star Tulip - Calochortus macrocarpus   MVW

PLATE 40   Golden Bowl – Calochortus clavatus   MVW

PLATE 41　Red Mariposa - Calochortus kennedyi　MVW

PLATE 42   Weed's Mariposa - Calochortus weedii   MVW

PLATE 43   Blue Dicks - Dichelostemma pauciflorum   MVW

PLATE 44   *Wild Onion - Allium cernuum*   MVW

PLATE 45   *Wild Chives - Allium sibiricum*   MVW

PLATE 46   Spanish Bayonet, Soapweed - Yucca navajoa   MVW

PLATE 47   *Bellwort - Uvularia perfoliata*   MVW

PLATE 48   *Blue Bead - Clintonia borealis*   MVW

PLATE 49   Queen Cup, Bride's Bonnet - Clintonia uniflora   MVW

PLATE 50   Queen Cup, Bride's Bonnet - Clintonia uniflora   MVW

PLATE 51   False Solomon's Seal - Smilacina stellata   MVW

PLATE 52   Twisted-stalk - Streptopus amplexifolius   MVW

PLATE 53   Western Twisted-stalk - Streptopus curvipes   MVW

PLATE 54 Purple Trillium - Trillium erectum MVW

PLATE 55   *Purple Trillium (white form) - Trillium erectum*   MVW

PLATE 56   *Trillium – Trillium grandiflorum*   MVW

PLATE 57   *Painted Trillium - Trillium undulatum*   MVW

PLATE 58   Toadshade - Trillium sessile   MVW

PLATE 59 Giant Trillium - Trillium chloropetalum MVW

PLATE 60   Atamasco Lily - Zephyranthes atamasco   MVW

PLATE 61   Spider Lily - *Hymenocallis rotata*   MVW

PLATE 62   Star Grass - Hypoxis hirsuta   DFP

PLATE 63   Blue-eyed Grass - Sisyrinchium angustifolium   MVW

PLATE 61   Large Blue Flag - Iris versicolor   MVW

PLATE 65   Dwarf Iris - Iris verna   MVW

PLATE 66   Crested Dwarf Iris - Iris cristata   MVW

PLATE 67   *Ram's-head Lady's-slipper - Cypripedium arietinum*   MVW

PLATE 68   *Yellow Lady's-slipper - Cypripedium calceolus*   MVW

PLATE 69   Showy Lady's-slipper - Cypripedium reginae   MVW

PLATE 70   *Mountain Lady's-slipper - Cypripedium montanum*   MVW

PLATE 71   *Pink Moccasin-flower - Cypripedium acaule*   MVW

PLATE 72   Pink Mocassin-flower - Cypripedium acaule   MVW

PLATE 73   Showy Orchis - Orchis spectabilis   MVW

PLATE 74   Round-leaved Orchis - Orchis rotundifolia   MVW

PLATE 75   Orange-plume - Habenaria ciliaris   MVW

PLATE 76   Ragged Orchid - Habenaria lacera   MVW

PLATE 77   *Purple Fringed Orchis - Habenaria psycodes*   MVW

PLATE 78   One-leaved Rein-orchis - Habenaria obtusata   MVW

PLATE 79   Heart-leaved Twayblade - Listera cordata   MVW

PLATE 80   Rosebud Orchid – Cleistes divaricata   MVW

PLATE 81   *Rose Pogonia - Pogonia ophioglossoides*   MVW

PLATE 82   Arethusa - Arethusa bulbosa   MVW

PLATE 83   Grass-pink - Calopogon pulchellus   MVW

PLATE 84   *Hooded Ladies' Tresses - Spiranthes romanzoffiana*   MVW

PLATE 85   *Nodding Ladies' Tresses - Spiranthes cernua*   MVW

Slender Ladies' Tresses - Spiranthes gracilis

PLATE 86   *Rattlesnake Plantain - Goodyera oblongifolia*   MVW

PLATE 87   *Calypso, Cytherea - Calypso bulbosa*   MVW

PLATE 88   *Twayblade - Liparis liliifolia*   MVW

PLATE 89   Butterfly Orchid - Epidendrum tampense   MVW

PLATE 90   Night-smelling Epidendrum - Epidendrum nocturnum   MVW

PLATE 91   Bee-swarm or Cowhorn Orchid - Cyrtopodium punctatum   MVW

PLATE 92   Pussy Willow - Salix discolor   MVW

PLATE 93   Drummond's Willow - Salix drummondiana   MVW

PLATE 96   *Mountain Alder - Alnus sinuata*   MVW

PLATE 97　　Bastard Toad-flax - Comandra livida　　MVW

PLATE 98   Mistletoe - Phoradendron flavescens   MVW

PLATE 99   Wild Ginger - Asarum canadense   MVW

PLATE 100   *Strawberry Blite - Chenopodium capitatum*   MVW

PLATE 101   Nodding Campion - Lychnis apetala   MVW

PLATE 102   Wild Pink - Silene caroliniana   MVW

PLATE 103   Moss Campion - Silene acaulis   MVW

PLATE 105   *Naiad Spring Beauty - Montia parvifolia*   MVW

PLATE 106   Water-lily - Nymphaea odorata   MVW

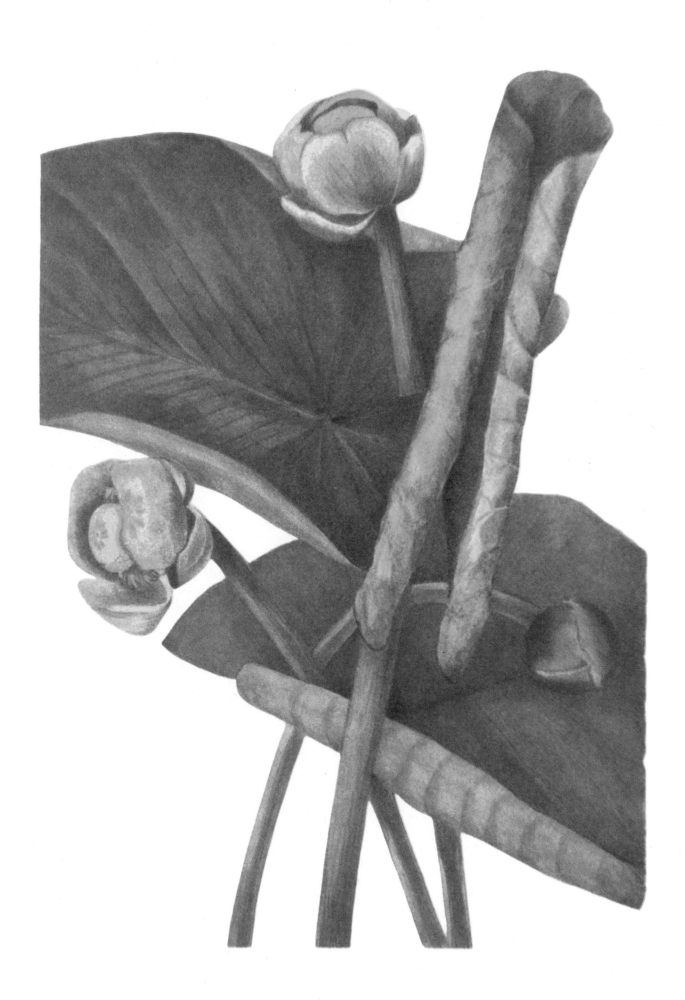

PLATE 107   Yellow Pond-lily - Nuphar advena   MVW

PLATE 110 Marsh Marigold, Cowslip - Caltha palustris   MVW

PLATE III   Columbine - Aquilegia canadensis   MVW

PLATE 112   *Yellow Columbine - Aquilegia flavescens*   MVW

PLATE 113   Shortspur Columbine - Aquilegia brevistyla   MVW

PLATE 114   Tall Larkspur - Delphinium elongatum   MVW

PLATE 115   Dwarf Larkspur - Delphinium depauperatum   MVW

PLATE 116   Western Red Baneberry - Actaea arguta   MVW

PLATE 117   Tall Buttercup - Ranunculus acris   DFP

PLATE 118   Avalanche Buttercup - Ranunculus suksdorfii   MVW

PLATE 119   Rue Anemone - Anemonella thalictroides   MVW

PLATE 120   *Columbia Windflower - Anemone deltoidea*   MVW

PLATE 121   Globose Anemone - Anemone globosa   MVW

PLATE I22   *Northern Anemone - Anemone parviflora*   MVW

PLATE 123   *Pasqueflower - Pulsatilla ludoviciana*   MVW

PLATE 124   Pasqueflower - Pulsatilla ludoviciana   MVW

PLATE 125   Western Pasqueflower - Pulsatilla occidentalis   MVW

PLATE 126   Western Pasqueflower - Pulsatilla occidentalis   MVW

PLATE 127   Hepatica - Hepatica americana   MVW

PLATE 128   *Blue Jasmine - Clematis crispa*   MVW

PLATE 129   *Virgin's Bower - Clematis columbiana*   MVW

PLATE 130   Virgin's Bower - Clematis columbiana   MVW

PLATE 131   Leather Flower - Clematis viorna   MVW

PLATE 132 Sweet Bay - Magnolia virginiana MVW

PLATE 133   Southern Magnolia - Magnolia grandiflora   MVW

PLATE 134   Southern Magnolia - Magnolia grandiflora   MVW

PLATE 135   *Cucumber Tree - Magnolia acuminata*   MVW

PLATE 136   Yellow Cucumber Tree - Magnolia cordata   MVW

PLATE 137   Tulip Tree, Yellow Poplar - Liriodendron tulipifera   MVW

PLATE 138   *Papaw – Asimina triloba*   MVW

PLATE 139   Creeping Mahonia - Mahonia repens   MVW

PLATE 140   Twinleaf - Jeffersonia diphylla   MVW

PLATE 141 *May-apple - Podophyllum peltatum* MVW

PLATE 142   *Mexican Poppy - Eschscholtzia mexicana*   MVW

PLATE 143   Bush Poppy - Dendromecon rigida   MVW

PLATE 144   *Bloodroot - Sanguinaria canadensis*   MVW

PLATE 145   *Pale Corydalis - Corydalis sempervirens*   MVW

PLATE 146   Squirrel Corn - Dicentra canadensis   MVW

PLATE 147   *Dutchman's Breeches – Dicentra cucullaria*   MVW

PLATE 148   Toothwort - Dentaria laciniata   MVW

PLATE 149   *Bladder-pod - Physaria didymocarpa*   MVW

PLATE 150   Bladder-pod - Physaria didymocarpa   MVW

PLATE 151   *Pitcher-plant - Sarracenia purpurea*   MVW

PLATE 152   Sweet Pitcher-plant - Sarracenia rubra   MVW

PLATE 153   *Hybrid Pitcher-plant - Sarracenia catesbaei*   MVW

PLATE 154   *Purple-trumpet - Sarracenia drummondii*   MVW

PLATE 155   *Yellow Pitcher-plant — Sarracenia flava*   MVW

PLATE 156   Hooded Pitcher-plant - Sarracenia minor   MVW

PLATE 157   *Parrot Pitcher-plant - Sarracenia psittacina*   MVW

PLATE 158   *Cobra Plant - Chrysamphora californica*   MVW

PLATE 159   *Venus' Fly-trap – Dionaea muscipula*   MVW

PLATE 160   *Fringed Parnassia - Parnassia fimbriata*   MVW

PLATE 165   *Prickly Currant - Ribes lacustre*   MVW

PLATE 166   *Prickly Currant - Ribes lacustre*   MVW

PLATE 167   Witch Hazel - Hamamelis virginiana   MVW

PLATE 168 *Hardhack - Spiraea tomentosa* DFP

PLATE 169   Bowman's Root - Gillenia trifoliata   MVW

PLATE 170   *Shrubby Cinquefoil - Potentilla fruticosa*   MVW

PLATE 171   Glaucous Cinquefoil - Potentilla glaucophylla   MVW

PLATE 174   *White Dryad - Dryas octopetala*   MVW

PLATE 175   *Yellow Dryad - Dryas drummondii*   MVW

PLATE 176   *Yellow Dryad - Dryas drummondii*   MVW

PLATE 177 *Prairie Smoke - Sieversia triflora* MVW

PLATE 178   Pale-leaved Strawberry - Fragaria glauca   MVW

PLATE 179   *Thimbleberry - Rubus parviflorus*   MVW

PLATE 180   *Flowering Raspberry - Rubus odoratus*   DFP

PLATE 181   Highbush Blackberry - Rubus argutus   MVW

PLATE 182   Red Dewberry - Rubus pedatus   MVW

PLATE 183   *Chickasaw Plum - Prunus angustifolia*   MVW

PLATE 184   Wild Rose - Rosa bourgeauiana   MVW

PLATE 185   Wild Rose - Rosa bourgeauiana   MVW

PLATE 186   Red Chokeberry - Aronia arbutifolia   MVW

PLATE 187   Red Chokeberry – Aronia arbutifolia   MVW

PLATE 188   Wild Sweet Crab - Malus coronaria   MVW

PLATE 189 Western Mountain Ash - Sorbus scopulina MVW

PLATE 190 Service-berry, Shad-bush - Amelanchier alnifolia   MVW

PLATE 191   *Partridge-pea - Cassia fasciculata*   DFP

PLATE 192   Redbud - Cercis canadensis   MVW

PLATE 193   *Wild Lupine - Lupinus perennis*   MVW

PLATE 194   *Prairie Clover - Petalostemum purpureum*   MVW

PLATE 195   Golden Pea - Thermopsis rhombifolia   MVW

PLATE 196   Goat's Rue - Tephrosia virginiana   MVW

PLATE 197   Milk-vetch - Astragalus bourgovii   MVW

PLATE 198   Alpine Milk-vetch - Astragalus alpinus   MVW

PLATE 199 *False Loco-weed - Oxytropis gracilis* MVW

PLATE 200   *Showy Oxytropis - Oxytropis splendens*   MVW

PLATE 201   *Point Vetch - Oxytropis podocarpa*   MVW

PLATE 202   *Point Vetch - Oxytropis podocarpa*   MVW

PLATE 203 *Wisteria - Wisteria frutescens* MVW

PLATE 204   Sweet Vetch - Hedysarum mackenzii   MVW

PLATE 205   Vetch - Vicia americana   MVW

PLATE 206   *Vetchling - Lathyrus ochroleucus*   MVW

PLATE 207   *Wild Geranium, Cranesbill - Geranium maculatum*   DFP

PLATE 208   Western Cranesbill - Geranium viscosissimum   MVW

PLATE 209   *Orange Milkwort - Polygala lutea*   MVW

PLATE 210   *Fringed Milkwort - Polygala paucifolia*   MVW

PLATE 211   *Crowberry - Empetrum nigrum*   MVW

PLATE 212   American Holly - Ilex opaca   MVW

PLATE 213   Yaupon, Cassena - Ilex vomitoria   MVW

PLATE 214   Winterberry - Ilex verticillata   MVW

PLATE 215   Red Maple - Acer rubrum   MVW

PLATE 216   Carolina Maple - Acer carolinianum   MVW

PLATE 217   Red Buckeye - Aesculus pavia   MVW

PLATE 218   Jewelweed, Touch-me-not - Impatiens capensis   DFP

PLATE 219 — Scarlet Globe-mallow — Malvastrum grossulariaefolium — MVW

PLATE 220   Globe-mallow - Sphaeralcea davidsonii   MVW

PLATE 221   Rose Mallow - Hibiscus moscheutos   DFP

PLATE 222 Tall St. John's Wort - *Hypericum pyramidatum*   DFP

PLATE 223 *Mexican Fremontia - Fremontia mexicana* MVW

PLATE 224   *Franklinia - Franklinia alatamaha*   MVW

PLATE 225   Stewartia - Stewartia malacodendron   MVW

PLATE 226   *Birdfoot Violet - Viola pedata*   MVW

PLATE 227   *Southern Coast Violet - Viola septemloba*   MVW

PLATE 228   *Canada Violet - Viola canadensis*   MVW

PLATE 229   *Smooth Yellow Violet - Viola eriocarpa*   MVW

PLATE 232   *Maypops - Passiflora incarnata*   MVW

PLATE 233 *Prickly Pear - Opuntia polyacantha*   MVW

PLATE 234   Strawberry Cactus - Echinocereus lloydii   MVW

PLATE 235   Green-flowered Strawberry Cactus - Echinocereus viridiflorus   MVW

PLATE 236   *Buffalo Berry - Shepherdia canadensis*   MVW

PLATE 237   Silverberry - Elaeagnus commutata   MVW

PLATE 238   Silverberry - Elaeagnus commutata   MVW

PLATE 239   *Evening Primrose - Oenothera biennis*   DFP

PLATE 240   *Evening Primrose - Pachylophus hirsutus*   MVW

PLATE 241   *Rock Rose - Pachylophus caespitosus*   MVW

PLATE 242   Fireweed - Epilobium angustifolium   MVW

PLATE 243 *Broad-leaved Willow-herb - Epilobium latifolium*   MVW

PLATE 244   Yellow Willow-herb - Epilobium luteum   MVW

PLATE 245   Devil's Club - Oplopanax horridus   MVW

PLATE 246   *Red-osier Dogwood - Cornus stolonifera*   MVW

PLATE 247   Flowering Dogwood - Cornus florida   MVW

PLATE 248   *Flowering Dogwood - Cornus florida*   MVW

PLATE 249   Bunchberry, Dwarf Cornel - Cornus canadensis   MVW

PLATE 250   Bunchberry, Dwarf Cornel - Cornus canadensis   MVW

PLATE 251   Labrador Tea - Ledum groenlandicum   MVW

PLATE 252   *Tar-flower – Befaria racemosa*   MVW

PLATE 253   Rose Bay - Rhododendron maximum   MVW

PLATE 254 *White-flowered Rhododendron - Rhododendron albiflorum* MVW

PLATE 255 Smooth Azalea - Rhododendron arborescens MVW

PLATE 256   *Pinkster-flower - Rhododendron nudiflorum*   MVW

PLATE 257   Mountain Azalea - Rhododendron roseum   MVW

PLATE 258   Flame Azalea - Rhododendron calendulaceum   MVW

PLATE 259   Pink-shell Azalea - Rhododendron vaseyi   MVW

PLATE 260   *Rhodora - Rhododendron canadense*   MVW

PLATE 261   Western Menziesia - Menziesia glabella   MVW

PLATE 262   Mountain Laurel - Kalmia latifolia   MVW

PLATE 263   *Bog Laurel - Kalmia polifolia*   MVW

PLATE 264   *Lambkill - Kalmia angustifolia*   MVW

PLATE 265   *Small-leaved Laurel - Kalmia microphylla*   MVW

PLATE 266   *Pink Mountain Heather - Phyllodoce empetriformis*   MVW

PLATE 267   *Zenobia - Zenobia cassinefolia*   MVW

PLATE 268   *Western Mountain Heather - Cassiope mertensiana*   MVW

PLATE 269   *Trailing Arbutus, Mayflower - Epigaea repens*   MVW

PLATE 270   Bearberry - Arctostaphylos uva-ursi   MVW

PLATE 271   Bearberry - Arctostaphylos uva-ursi   MVW

PLATE 272   *Ptarmigan-berry - Arctostaphylos alpina*   MVW

PLATE 273   *Pipsissewa, Prince's Pine - Chimaphila umbellata*   MVW

PLATE 274   *One-flowered Wintergreen - Moneses uniflora*   MVW

PLATE 275   Green Pyrola, Shinleaf - Pyrola virens   MVW

PLATE 276   Small Pyrola, Shinleaf - Pyrola minor   MVW

PLATE 277   *Sidebells Pyrola - Pyrola secunda*   MVW

PLATE 278   *Indian Pipe - Monotropa uniflora*   MVW

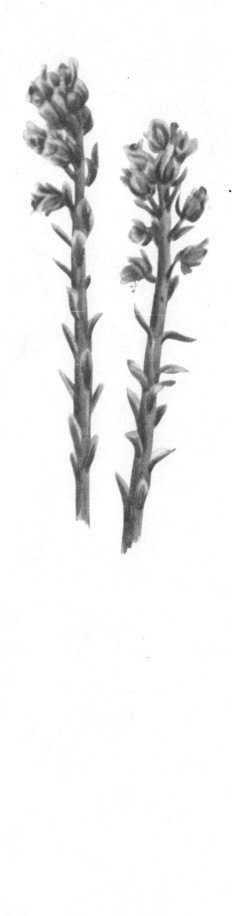

PLATE 279   *Pinesap - Hypopitys monotropa*   MVW

PLATE 280   *Red Pinesap - Hypopitys lanuginosa*   MVW

PLATE 281 Box Huckleberry - Gaylussacia brachycera MVW

PLATE 282   Deerberry - Polycodium stamineum   MVW

PLATE 283   *Highbush Blueberry - Vaccinium corymbosum*   MVW

PLATE 284   *Pineland Blueberry - Vaccinium tenellum*   MVW

PLATE 287   Oconee-bells - Shortia galacifolia   MVW

PLATE 288   *Pyxie - Pyxidanthera barbulata*   MVW

PLATE 289   *Pigmy Androsace - Androsace subumbellata*   MVW

PLATE 290   *Sweet Androsace - Androsace carinata*   MVW

PLATE 291   *Bird's-eye Primrose - Primula mistassinica*   MVW

PLATE 292   Shooting-star - Dodecatheon meadia   MVW

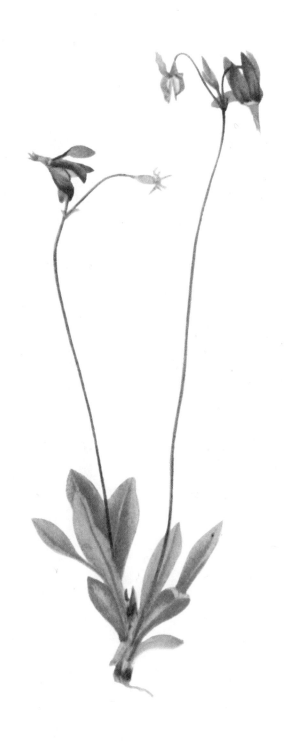

PLATE 293   Slender Shooting-star – Dodecatheon pauciflorum   MVW

PLATE 294   *Fringe-tree - Chionanthus virginiana*   MVW

PLATE 295 *Carolina Jessamine - Gelsemium sempervirens* MVW

PLATE 296   *Felwort - Gentiana amarella*   MVW

PLATE 297   Fringed Gentian - Gentiana crinita   MVW

PLATE 298   Pine-barren Gentian - Gentiana porphyrio   MVW

PLATE 299   *Bottle Gentian, Soapwort - Gentiana saponaria*   MVW

PLATE 300   *Ruff Gentian - Gentiana calycosa*   MVW

PLATE 301   *Prairie Gentian - Gentiana affinis*   MVW

PLATE 302   *Blue-green Gentian - Gentiana glauca*   MVW

PLATE 303 Salt-marsh Rose-gentian - Sabbatia stellaris   MVW

PLATE 304   Pink Centaury - Centaurium venustum   MVW

PLATE 305   Bogbean, Buckbean - Menyanthes trifoliata   MVW

PLATE 306   Showy Milkweed - *Asclepias speciosa*   MVW

PLATE 307   *Butterfly-weed - Asclepias tuberosa*   MVW

PLATE 308   Wild Sweet William - Phlox divaricata   MVW

PLATE 309   Jacob's Ladder, Greek Valerian - Polemonium reptans   DFP

PLATE 310   *Ocotillo - Fouquieria splendens*   MVW

PLATE 311   Sand Phacelia - Phacelia linearis   MVW

PLATE 312   Silky Phacelia - Phacelia sericea   MVW

PLATE 313   Mistmaiden - Romanzoffia sitchensis   MVW

PLATE 314   Bluebell, Virginia Cowslip - Mertensia virginica   MVW

PLATE 315   Tall Lungwort - Mertensia paniculata   MVW

PLATE 316   Moss Forget-me-not - Eritrichium elongatum   MVW

PLATE 317   Bur Forget-me-not - Lappula diffusa   MVW

PLATE 318   Alpine Forget-me-not - Myosotis alpestris   MVW

PLATE 319   *Verbena - Verbena canadensis*   DFP

PLATE 320   French Mulberry, Beautyberry - Callicarpa americana   MVW

PLATE 321   Skullcap - Scutellaria serrata   MVW

PLATE 322   Horsemint - Monarda punctata   MVW

PLATE 323   *Beebalm, Oswego Tea - Monarda didyma*   DFP

PLATE 324   Monkey-flower - Mimulus guttatus   MVW

PLATE 325   Scarlet Monkey-flower - Mimulus cardinalis   MVW

PLATE 326   *Lewis' Monkey-flower - Mimulus lewisii*   MVW

PLATE 327   Alpine Monkey-flower - Mimulus caespitosus   MVW

PLATE 328　　*Bush Monkey-flower - Diplacus longiflorus*　　MVW

PLATE 329   Red Monkey-flower - Diplacus puniceus   MVW

PLATE 330   *Turtlehead - Chelone glabra*   MVW

PLATE 331   Foxglove Penstemon – Penstemon digitalis   MVW

PLATE 332   *Prairie Beard-tongue - Penstemon eriantherus*   MVW

PLATE 333 *Fire Penstemon - Penstemon eatoni* MVW

PLATE 334   Lyall's Penstemon - Penstemon lyallii   MVW

PLATE 335   Rock Penstemon - Penstemon rupicola   MVW

PLATE 336 Desert Penstemon - Penstemon parryi MVW

PLATE 337   *Blue-eyed Mary - Colinsia verna*   MVW

PLATE 338 Butter-and-eggs, Toadflax - Linaria vulgaris DFP

PLATE 339 *False Foxglove - Aureolaria virginica* DFP

PLATE 340   Red Helmet - Pedicularis bracteosa   MVW

PLATE 341   *Alpine Fern-leaf - Pedicularis contorta*   MVW

PLATE 342   *Elephant-head - Pedicularis groenlandica*   MVW

PLATE 343   Owl Clover - Orthocarpus tenuifolius   MVW

PLATE 344 *Indian Paintbrush - Castilleia miniata* MVW

PLATE 345   *Pale Paintbrush - Castilleia pallida*   MVW

PLATE 346   Lance-leaf Paintbrush - Castilleia lancifolia   MVW

PLATE 349   *Cancer-root - Orobanche uniflora*   MVW

PLATE 350   *Squaw-root - Conopholis americana*   MVW

PLATE 351   Trumpet Creeper - Campsis radicans   MVW

PLATE 352   *Cross-vine - Anisostichus capreolatus*   MVW

PLATE 353   Bedstraw – Galium boreale   MVW

PLATE 354   *Bluets, Quaker Ladies - Houstonia caerulea*   MVW

PLATE 355   *Partridge-berry - Mitchella repens*   MVW

PLATE 356 Squashberry, Cranberry-bush - *Viburnum pauciflorum* MVW

PLATE 357   Red-berried Elder - Sambucus pubens   MVW

PLATE 358   Honeysuckle - Lonicera glaucescens   MVW

PLATE 359   Honeysuckle - Lonicera glaucescens   MVW

PLATE 360   *Bearberry Honeysuckle - Lonicera involucrata*   MVW

PLATE 361　　*Trumpet Honeysuckle - Lonicera sempervirens*　　MVW

PLATE 362   Twinflower - Linnaea borealis   MVW

PLATE 363   *Valerian - Valeriana sitchensis*   MVW

PLATE 366   Brook Lobelia - Lobelia kalmii   MVW

PLATE 367 Cardinal Flower - Lobelia cardinalis MVW

PLATE 368   Black-eyed Susan - Rudbeckia hirta   DFP

PLATE 369   Sunflower - Helianthus strumosus   DFP

PLATE 370   Balsam-root - Balsamorhiza sagittata   MVW

PLATE 371   Golden Star - Chrysogonum virginianum   MVW

PLATE 372   *Perennial Gaillardia - Gaillardia aristata*   MVW

PLATE 373   Yarrow - Achillea lanulosa   MVW

PLATE 374   New England Aster - Aster novae-angliae   DFP

PLATE 375   Pineland Aster - Aster walteri   MVW

PLATE 376   *Prairie Aster - Aster campestris*   MVW

PLATE 377   *Fleabane - Erigeron peregrinus*   MVW

PLATE 378   Meadow Fleabane - Erigeron speciosus   MVW

PLATE 379 *Fleabane - Erigeron caespitosus* MVW

PLATE 380   Golden Fleabane - Erigeron aureus   MVW

PLATE 381   Aleutian Fleabane - Erigeron humilis   MVW

PLATE 382   Goldenrod - Solidago canadensis   DFP

PLATE 384   *Pearly Everlasting – Anaphalis margaritacea*   MVW

PLATE 385   *Pink Everlasting - Antennaria rosea*   MVW

PLATE 386   *Howell's Everlasting - Antennaria howellii*   MVW

PLATE 387   *Brown Everlasting - Antennaria luzuloides*   MVW

PLATE 388   Woolly Arnica - Arnica tomentosa   MVW

PLATE 389   Lake Louise Arnica - Arnica louiseana   MVW

PLATE 390   Mourning Ragwort - Senecio lugens   MVW

PLATE 391   Few-flowered Groundsel - Senecio pauciflorus   MVW

PLATE 392   *Arrow-leaf Ragwort - Senecio triangularis*   MVW

PLATE 393   *Butterbur - Petasites hyperboreus*   MVW

PLATE 394   Joe-Pye Weed - Eupatorium purpureum   DFP

PLATE 395   *White Thistle - Cirsium hookerianum*   MVW

PLATE 396   Wavy-leaved or Prairie-Thistle - Cirsium undulatum   MVW

PLATE 397　　Saussurea - Saussurea densa　　MVW

PLATE 398   Slender Agoseris - Agoseris gracilens   MVW

PLATE 399   *Grass-leaved Agoseris - Agoseris graminifolia*   MVW

PLATE 400   Woolly Agoseris - Agoseris villosa   MVW